MW01504546

VALENTINA GENTILE

From Identity-Conflict to Civil Society

Restoring Human Dignity and Pluralism in Deeply Divided Societies

Foreword by Sebastiano Maffettone
Post-scriptum by Neera Chandhoke

© 2012 Luiss University Press – Pola s.r.l. a socio unico
All rights reserved
ISBN 978-88-6105-158-4

1st edition: november, 2012
2nd edition revised and expanded: february, 2013

Luiss University Press – Pola s.r.l.
Viale Pola, 12
00198 Roma
Tel.06 85225485
Fax 06 85225236
www.luissuniversitypress.it
e-mail lup@luiss.it

Progetto grafico e impaginazione: HaunagDesign

For my parents, Gino and Ester,
and for me

Table of Contents

List of figures and tables

List of abbreviations

ARBiH	Armija Republike BiH
	(Army of the Republic of Bosnia Herzegovina)
ARMP	Associations of Relatives of Missing Persons
AVIDP	Associations of Victims, Inmates, and Displaced Persons
BiH	Bosna i Hercegovina (Bosnia-Herzegovina)
CSOs	Civil Society Organizations
CCT	Contemporary Conflict Theories
FBiH	Federacije Bosne i Hercegovine
	(Federation of Bosnia-Herzegovina)
FCMP	Federal Commission for Missing Persons
HDZ	Hrvatska Demokratska Zajednica (Croatian Democratic Union)
HVO	Hrvatsko Vijeće Obrane (Croat Defense Army)
ICG	International Crisis Group
ICMP	International Commission for Missing Persons
ICRC	International Committee of the Red Cross
ICTY	International Criminal Tribunal for the former Yugoslavia
INGOs	International Non-governmental Organizations
NGOs	Non-governmental Organizations
OTDMPRS	Office for Tracing Detained and Missing Persons
	of Republic of Srpska
OHR	Office of the High Representative
OSCE	Organization for Security and Cooperation in Europe
PSC	Protracted Social Conflict Theory
RS	Republika Srpska (Srpska Republic)
SDS	Srpska Demokratska Stranka (Serb Democratic Party)
UN	United Nations
UNHCR	United Nation High Commissioner for Refugees
VRS	Vojska Republike Srpske (Army of the RS)

Foreword

by Sebastiano Maffettone

Contemporary wars, if compared to traditional "Westphalian" wars, present an evident characteristic: often they are *civil* or *internal* rather than *interstate* or *external* wars. This means that in all these conflicts civil society is the core element and the main subject. This is true of the period, from 1989 onwards, when the so-called "identity politics" has played a fundamental role. It is almost commonsensical today to claim that in the last two decades identity politics has taken the position once held by economic issues in most social conflicts. Such conflicts have taken place in countries like Bosnia, Kosovo, Sri Lanka, East Timor, and their roots are ethnic or religious.

Given this background, it is both necessary and natural to look for a political theory able to treat conflicts connected with identity politics in the perspective of the civil society. *From Identity-Conflict to Civil Society* by Valentina Gentile aims to understand the complex dynamics related to civil society in fragmented societies from one specific standpoint – the identity of the persons involved in the conflicts. In particular, the book investigates the way in which several civil society organizations intervene in ethno-religious conflicts in the light of pluralism of values. It is also enriched by an empirical counterpart, so unusual within the domain of political philosophy, on civil society in Bosnia after the Dayton talks. This empirical section however is not meant to be an independent aspect of the investigation, but a further element to better settle and understand the sophisticated normative core of the book. The output of the analysis is framed within the scheme of global justice, on which the Centre on Ethics and Global Politics at LUISS University in Rome – coordinated by Valentina Gentile herself – has been concentrating its efforts during the last years. That is why the major result of the normative political theoretical inquiry is in terms of human rights protection and democratic transition.

Although in recent years many works have been published treating ethno-religious conflicts and civil society, this book represents a very original contribution to the academic debate in this field for at least two reasons. First, in literature, only a few systematic attempts have been made to connect these two features. Second, as far as I know, this is the first book that treats this subject from the point of view of a normative political philosophy inspired by liberalism. This confirms the significance and the absolute relevance of Gentile's book within the panorama of contemporary political theory. I myself know by personal acquaintance how much work was needed to produce such a book. It was originated by Valentina Gentile's Ph.D. thesis, under my supervision, and required many years of further research and teaching (on related subjects) to take the present form. For all these reasons it is my deep conviction that readers and critics will give it the most serious consideration.

Acknowledgements

I have been studying and reading about these issues — identity in conflict, civil society and reconciliation — for a number of years during and after my Ph.D. However, most of this work has been written during 2007 and 2008. I spent this period in Italy at the Centre for Ethics and Global Politics (ex CERSDU) at Luiss University of Rome, and in the Netherlands where I was Marie Curie Research Fellow at the Centre for Conflict Studies at Utrecht University. Both periods have been very fruitful for my work and I should mention with gratitude all those friends, colleagues and professors who read and encouraged me in my project.

First, I am grateful to my mentor and good friend, Sebastiano Maffettone, for his always-helpful support and encouragement during all these years. Sebastiano gave me the chance to carry out this work, following with care, affection and, sometimes, patience, my intellectual and scholarly development all these years. My thanks go, then, to my colleague Aakash Singh Rathore, not only for his support and suggestions to improve several versions of this work, but also for the friendship he has shown me on many occasions all these years. Gratitude is also due to other colleagues and friends at Luiss who helped me in reconsidering several preliminary ideas of my work; many thanks to Gianfranco Pellegrino, Daniele Santoro, Tom Bailey, Michele Bocchiola, Serena Ciccarelli, Marcello Di Paola and Domenico Melidoro. Also, I would like to thank all the international guests who visited our centre in the last few years; through several discussions and colloquia I was able to develop and specify some important sections of this work. In particular, I would like to thank Neera Chandhoke for the long conversations about our common research interests, but also for her friendship and care. Finally, I am indebted to Professor Will Kymlicka for his valuable comments and his constructive criticisms to the idea of 'culture of civility'.

My profound thanks to Jolle Demmers who enthusiastically supervised my work at the Center for Conflict at Utrecht. The six months I spent in Utrecht allowed me to study conflicts in a multidisciplinary environment, in addition to readings and discussions with colleagues and professors at the Centre prepared by me for the case study in Bosnia. I am also indebted to Roberto Belloni and Lorenza Fabretti for the long conversations and their helpful suggestions. Finally, I should mention that the case study was part of a broader case-study work organized in the framework of the VI Framework Research Program Shur 'Human rights in conflict: the role of civil society'. From 2006 to 2009 I was a member of the research team of the Shur programme. I should then thank the coordinators of this programme, Raffaele Marchetti and Nathalie Tocci, and all the members of the research team for their invaluable suggestions and comments and the exchange of thoughts we had during the years of the project.

From 2009 to 2012 my work has been further revised and I gave new emphasis to political normative theory with special attention to the ideas of consensus and reconciliation in deeply divided societies. These new ideas contributed to specify the meaning of 'culture of civility', which I included in this last version of the book. In this respect, I am indebted to Albert Weale and Richard Bellamy who generously invited me to spend time as a visiting researcher at the School of Public Policy, UCL, from January to March 2010. In April 2012, I presented a revised version of the idea of culture of civility at the UCSIA Lecture on Religion Politics and the State. I am grateful to Willem Lemmens and Walter Van Herck for their comments and support during the time I spent in Antwerp.

I am grateful to the Luiss administrative staff: in particular, I should mention Gaia Di Martino, Claudia Pannunzi, Maria Sole Micali, Antonella La Greca and Roberta Felici who have always supported and encouraged me in the past. I should also mention the work of Luiss University Press and, in particular, I am grateful to Matteo Rollier and Daniele Rosa for their support to this editorial project.

Last, but not least, I must mention all those people whose loving support made my work easier in Naples, Rome, Utrecht, London and Antwerp. Special thanks go therefore to my parents, my brother Christian and my sister Isa and all the good friends who have constantly supported and encouraged me in the last years. Finally, many thanks to the person who gave me new energies and enthusiasm in the last year. This is also for you.

One should not be afraid of humans.
Well, I am not afraid of the humans,
but of what is inhuman in them.

Ivo Andríc (1892-1975)
Nobel Prize in Literature in 1961

Introduction:
from identity-conflict to civil society

Recently, much scholarly work has been done on civil society and ethno-religious conflicts. Increasingly, social scientists, political theorists and anthropologists have emphasized the key role played by civil society actors in democratic transition, in particular with reference to contexts of deeply divided societies. However, only in a few cases have systematic attempts to connect the two been made, in general related to empirical researches.[1] This work is aimed at offering a multidisciplinary perspective of civil society and identity-conflicts based on a deeper understanding of the idea of individual identity. With respect to previous works, here the emphasis is placed on the theoretical analysis of these concepts, rather than on empirical investigations. Furthermore, unlike other attempts, this work is aimed at integrating different perspectives and disciplines in the framework of a philosophical investigation.

As a matter of fact, in the last two decades, two relevant phenomena have emerged and increasingly captured the interest of scholars.

First, the years after the Cold War have seen a shift in the number and typology of armed conflicts (Lederach 1997; Ramsbotham et al. 2006). In contexts like Bosnia, Kosovo, Sri Lanka and East Timor, the traditional understanding of conflict as international/interstate cannot grasp the complexity and explain the dynamics of such ethno-religious intrastate wars (Duffield 2001; Hartzell et al. 2001; Varshney 2001). The first relevant element regards their proportion; according to the traditional approach new conflicts would be classified as minor or intermediate armed conflicts (Wallensteen and Axell 1993; Wallensteen and Sollenberg 1999).[2] The second feature concerns their cultural matrix: fighting groups make use of identitarian arguments, whether constructed or givens, to mobilize people. Finally, a further aspect concerns the typology of the warring parties. Very often, they are irregular combatants or, as someone defines them, 'rebels' (Collier and Hoeffler 2004; Collier et al. 2006). Their emergence is mostly due to the weakness or absence of a legitimate state authority. Such contexts are characterized by widespread criminality, frequent violent and predatory actions directed against civilians and systematic violations of fundamental human rights.

In addition, in recent years, several varieties of different non-state actors have emerged. Religious and ethnical movements, local and international non-governmental organizations, and national and transnational social movements represent the renewed expression of civil society (Anheier et al. 2001; Cohen and Arato 1994). The impact of these actors seems to be more relevant in contexts where the vacuum deriving from the failure of the nation state model is more evident (Kaldor 1999). With reference to this, the context of identity-conflicts seems to be particularly significant. Actually, while the effectiveness of the traditional nation-state intervention in these conflicts decreases, an intimate link between civil society and these wars emerges. Most of the recent peace operations have seen the involvement of local and international civil society actors. Increasingly, both scholars and practitioners have shown their confidence in the positive role of civil society engagement in the post-conflict transition of deeply divided societies (Fetherston 1999; Lederach 1997, 2001).

The present book is aimed at understanding the complex dynamics related to civil society engagement in deeply divided societies. In particular, it explores the interrelations between civil society and conflicts, with particular attention to the impact of civil society on human rights protection and democratic transition. The work is based on three premises.

First, the massive and systematic violation of human rights is a key factor in the dynamics of the emerging ethno-religious conflicts.

Second, civil society organizations and movements intervene in various ways in such conflicts. Some further clarifications follow from this second issue. One can conceive of, at least, two levels of civil society engagement in conflict, namely the local and international dimensions of civil society's intervention.

(i) At the international level, there are organizations and movements, international non-governmental organizations (hereafter INGOs), engaged in actions such as humanitarian intervention, human rights protection, peace-building and democratic transition. Many authors emphasize the constructive potential of these actors in creating sustainable and stable peace (Lederach 1997, 2001; Fetherston 1999; Kaldor 2003a). According to them, these organizations are crucially important in both building democratic institutions and promoting liberal peace 'from the bottom' (Richmond and Carey 2005).

(ii) Nevertheless, other scholars discuss the ambivalent role of such an 'external' intervention in local deeply divided contexts (Paffenholz and Spurk 2006; Pouligny 2005). According to them, these actors very often lack concrete long-term strategies for fostering local inter-group cooperation and dialogue (Belloni

2001; Bieber 2002; Fisher 2006). However, although large number of studies have been written on the alleged positive impact of communal and local CSOs on multi-ethnic or multi-communal communities civil society's intervention appears controversial, also with regard to the local level, the local civil society organizations (henceforth CSOs). Many scholars emphasize the inclusive attitude of these actors in contexts of cultural violence and exclusion (Varshney 2003a); their efforts would be necessary to guarantee a genuine reconciliation among fighting groups and preserve an endogenous democratic development, based on trust, solidarity, and accountability (Belloni 2001; Pouligny 2005). Nevertheless, in spite of these positive premises, ambivalences and disintegrative potentials also emerge with respect to the local side of civil society. Some scholars refer to a kind of 'uncivil society', made up of criminal or extremist groups. According to them, especially when a state does not exist or it is failing, the boundaries between society's actors and groups (violent and non-violent) are more likely to vanish, and 'un-civil', xenophobic, or mafia-like groups may emerge (Anheier, Kaldor & Glasius 2006; Belloni 2006; Paffenholz & Spurk 2006). These movements would take part in the conflict alternately using different methods of action, from mobilization by means of media to open violence, as in the cases of ethnic cleansings and terrorist attacks.

Third, the protection of values such as human dignity and pluralism is seen as a necessary condition for peace and stability in war-torn societies. In this perspective, the protection of these values in the realm of civil society turns out to be the crucial factor for building human security and for fostering an autonomous democratic development.

In the present work, a theoretical framework for civil society engagement in post-conflict societies is formulated. Such an idea is rooted in two main assumptions. First, de-essentializing identity-conflicts means to seriously take into account an idea of multiple identities (Sen 2006a). Second, starting from an idea of society where individuals are linked to each other by virtue of their plural affiliations, I emphasize the necessity to understand civil society as a complex equilibrium among cultural, political and economic domains, where individual interests and pursuits meet collective claims and shared experiences. In this perspective, civil society is neither a sphere of the non-governmental sector, understood as an autonomous public sphere, nor a private sphere, as such. Following Hegel, it is possible to argue that civil society is the intermediate sphere existing between 'family' and 'state', where all those forms of economic linkages, associational modalities and cultural expressions come out. It represents the antistate, since there emerge all those forms that constitute a counterweight to the 'tyranny of the state' (Taylor 1995); but it also corresponds to a kind of 'anticipation' of the more extensive experience of the state. In this second sense, civil society is supposed to be the sphere where a shared 'culture of civility' emerges. I define 'culture of civility' as a specific kind of culture on which it is possible to build an autonomous democratic development of a society.

Finally, such an approach is tested to an actual case of post-conflict transition, the case of Bosnia-Herzegovina (hereafter Bosnia). With reference to this case, this approach is likely to emphasize the aspects of 'civility' already present in Bosnian society, such as non-violence, and protection of human dignity, which actually are part of the Bosnian 'culture of civility'.

The book comprises four chapters. The first chapter is meant to offer a general introduction to the theoretical issues discussed in the following chapters, which entail the concepts of identity-conflicts, democratic values such as human dignity and pluralism, and civil society. The second chapter is devoted to the analysis of contemporary ethno-religious conflicts in the light of the recent works in the literature on conflict studies. This chapter also presents a de-essentialized concept of identity applied to conflicts. The third chapter introduces the concept of civil society and the idea of civility related to it. The last chapter presents a case study on Bosnia.[3]

This second edition is revised and expanded to include a Post-Scriptum written by Professor Neera Chandhoke. In this commentary, Professor Chandhoke critically examines the notion of civil society as presented in this book and the idea of "culture of civility" related to it. In particular, the new section, which also comprises a reply to Chandhoke's commentary, aims at deepening the relation between the "culture of civility" and the legal institutional framework of the state.

NOTES

1. I am referring to scholars like Orjuela (2003) and Varshney (2003a) who have worked on Sri Lanka and India respectively.
2. According to these works, from 1989 to 2000, there were 111 armed conflicts in the world, of which 104 were intrastate conflicts; this means that civil wars accounted for 94 per cent of all armed conflicts.
3. This section is based on qualitative research carried out during a field trip in Bosnia from 30 November 2007 to 6 December 2007.

Chapter 1

Exploring the nexus:
identity-conflicts, human dignity, civil society

1.1 Identity-conflicts: deepening the meaning of identity in conflict – 1.2 Human rights in identity-conflicts: the meaning of 'human dignity' – 1.3 Civil society, identity-conflicts, and democratic transition: theoretical issues

1.1
IDENTITY-CONFLICTS: DEEPENING THE MEANING
OF IDENTITY IN CONFLICT

In 1990, the end of the Cold War, the collapse of the Soviet Union, the wave of democratization in Latin America and Eastern Europe, the crisis of many authoritarian regimes in Africa, all led to the illusory hope of democracy and freedom at the global level. The reality was in fact deeply different. Actually, the overcoming of the Cold War confrontation and the emergence of a globalized market made room for the intensification of social and political conflicts that contributed to deepen the crisis of the old Westphalian system of sovereign territorial states. Societies entered a period of painful social, economic and institutional transformation marked by dramatic security dilemmas. The growing weakness and the ineffectiveness of national institutions to represent public interests and to protect citizens multiplied the number of ethnic and cultural conflicts. The escalation of violence tremendously increased, both across boundaries and within failed states (Anheier and Albrow 2006).

The contemporary 'new wars' (Kaldor 1999) do not have an actual beginning or a formal end, furthermore it is too difficult, if not impossible, to establish a clear distinction between peace and war. These conflicts are fought by groups of states and non-state actors, such as para-military, rebel armies, child soldiers, or terrorist groups. Very often, the act of violence directed at civilians is the instrument of struggle *par excellence*. Most importantly, 'identity groups', namely ethnic, or religious groups, and not nation-states, are at the core of such conflicts.

Scholars from deeply different fields have increasingly paid attention to these conflicts. Kalyvas, a political scientist from Yale University, offers an interesting reading of this peculiar kind of 'civil war' (Kalyvas 2003, 2007). According to him, such conflicts can be described in the light of the interaction between political and private identities and actions. This suggests that master cleavages, of religious or ethnic matrix, would represent a sort of 'symbolic formation' (Kalyvas 2003: 486), which simplifies and encompasses several local conflicts. These local conflicts seem to be linked to peripheral or 'private issues' rather than collective public claims. However, several scholars are more likely to emphasize the collective character of these conflicts. Azar's (1990) theory on protracted social conflicts (hereafter, PSC) plays a pivotal role in this literature.

Azar's intuitions, developed in a vast series of publications over a 20-year period from the early-1970s (Ramsbotham 2005), about the relevance of grievances due to the deprivation of human needs in protracted internal conflict still represent a useful tool for understanding identity-conflicts. According to the PSC theory, the crucial factor in such deeply divided societies is represented by the prolonged and often violent struggle among communal groups for some basic human needs. He lists five fundamental needs, namely security, recognition, acceptance, fair access to political institutions and economic participation. According to his view, 'grievances resulting from need deprivation are usually expressed collectively. Failure to redress these grievances by the authority cultivates a niche for a protracted social conflict' (Azar 1990: 9). In other words, according to Azar the identitarian character of these wars is the result of the frustration resulting from needs deprivation.

From a general point of view, several questions are at issue with reference to such conflicts. What does identity mean? Why should the quest of recognition represent a fundamental human need? Furthermore, what is the role of individuals in such a frame? One can recognize two extreme positions regarding the idea of cultural identity in conflict (Sen 2006a, 2008). On the one hand, individualist reductionism shows a complete lack of interest about cultural identity. Following the contemporary economic and political approaches to conflicts, individuals are perceived as fundamental subjects of any political action.[1] Groups can only do things via individuals' actions. In such a frame, individuals' actions and choices are independent of the group and cultural identity becomes an irrelevant variable. On the other hand, cultural reductionism represents its opposite version. Such a reductionism considers that individuals are not separate units, but rather are part of a larger group (i.e. extended family, village, ethnic or religious community). According to supporters of PSC theory and other cultural reductionists, one cannot describe individuals' actions and motivations without considering the significance of their shared identities. In fact, both views are extremely dangerous and, what is more important, do not explain the content of identity and the significance of the quest of differentiation in contemporary divided societies.

The present work suggests a third way to look at the relation between identity and violence which relies on a more complex and de-essentialized understanding of identity, as it has been recently presented by philosophers like Amartya Sen and Anthony Appiah (Appiah 2007; Sen 2006a, 2008). The idea that individuals are independent islands is hardly acceptable in real life. Even if there are no doubts that these wars have an individualistic root, based on private interests and actions, nonetheless, it seems extremely difficult to isolate this element from the collective and ideological dimension of violence. At the same time, it would be inappropriate to argue that individuals' actions are deeply rooted in shared experiences within groups or communities. Such an emphasis on cultural differences among groups, rather than individuals, would lead to the extreme thesis that cultural heterogeneity itself is at the roots of violence (Huntington 1996).

It seems more plausible to argue that each individual holds a plurality of identities.[2] Ethnic as well as religious features represent only some attributions of our identity. A person recognizes herself or himself in terms of age, gender, profession, level of education, political ideology, religious beliefs, nationality, race, caste, and ethnic affiliations. It means that each individual is the result of a complex set of different identities. Individuals are not only rational; without considering the emotional side of their shared identities, it is difficult to understand the human experiences of people like Nelson Mandela, Mother Teresa, or Gandhi. However, the essentialist approach to identity is not less dangerous and unfruitful than the first form of reductionism. Now let's consider the example of Mother Teresa: her life can hardly be explained in rational terms, nonetheless it is abundantly clear that her religious affiliation, Christian Catholicism, is not enough to explain her experience as a missionary of charity. She used to define herself as a woman ('I am a woman'), as an Albanian ('by blood, I am Albanian') but also as an Indian by adoption ('by citizenship, an Indian'), as a catholic by faith ('By faith, I am a catholic nun') and — what is more important — as a part of the human community ('As to my calling, I belong to the world'). The combination of all these attributions makes Mother Teresa's experience so unique and unrepeatable.

Thus, the idea of multiple identities impresses upon us to understand how and why in new conflicts religious and ethnic features tend to overcome other attributions. The problem here is to understand how and why such identities interact with political violence. Neither ethnicity, nor race, nor religion can be considered as violent factors *per se*. According to the thesis of the plural affiliations, the fact that an individual is either black or white, Christian or Muslim, Croat or Serb, does not say anything about her/him; the combination of all different identities makes an individual and his/her human experience recognizable. If it is true that the evidence of contemporary conflicts seems to say that these factors are inherently violent, nevertheless, it would be misleading to take this assumption too seriously: the history of humanity starting from the Christian Crusades to Hitler's eugenic plan for a master race, is actually studded with examples of violence hidden behind cultures, religions and racial or ethnic features.

The link between identity and violence is therefore complex and, it is necessary for a political theorist to handle these categories cautiously. It is possible to distinguish two key factors: the role of recognition, on the one hand, and the idea of private interests and actions, on the other. The first issue is meant to emphasize the social grievances linked to the lack of recognition within society, which represents a fundamental *capability-deprivation* (Sen 1999). The second argument focuses on the demagogic use of *groups* and *groupness* as independent sources of violence. These two arguments are profoundly linked to each other; frequently, in contexts where the sense of frustration is high, due to the general condition of needs-deprivation, a specific kind of actors that I call *cultural-war-entrepreneurs* fuel violence reinventing the mythology of the losers for hiding their actual interests and purposes.

The frustration and the sense of deprivation emerging from the lack of recognition of some identities plays a key role in these conflicts, but ethnic or religious heterogeneity does not represent *per se* an obstacle to peace and stability.[3] The lack of security experienced in deeply divided societies is rather related to the levels of people's capabilities, tolerance and acceptance of diversity within society. Very often, in conflict situations, the condition of *capability-deprivation* translates into the refusal to recognize or accept the ethnic or religious attributions of others. Such a condition increases the levels of social grievances, exclusion and marginalization within society. Societies are redesigned in terms of losers and winners, marginalized and not. The sense of revenge and frustration that follows such a denial of *substantive freedoms* (Sen 1999) represents an important factor in motivating violent social struggles.

Additionally, it is necessary to distinguish such attributions as religion, race or ethnicity, from individuals' interests and actions. Often, the earlier mentioned sense of revenge is employed as a 'public justification' by private groups or, simply, self-interested individuals to get some public support. In this respect, the sociologist Brubaker has made an interesting distinction between group as a category and group as an organization. In conflict situations, he argues, 'although participants' rhetoric and common-sense accounts treat ethnic groups as the protagonists of most ethnic conflict, in fact the chief protagonist of most ethnic [...] violence are not groups as such but various kind of organizations' (Brubaker 2004: 41). Such a distinction between groups and organizations is meant to trace a clear difference between the quest of recognition and the use that some self-interested groups can make of such a demand. The war creates communities of fear. New actors — that I call 'cultural-war-entrepreneurs' — intervene in the public arena articulating their own mythology of the conflict, starting from features such as religion, ethnicity or nation that differentiate each community from each other. Such a demagogic use of the argument of recognition depends, on the one hand, on the thuggish interests and grim purposes of a few individuals that find it convenient to manipulate the conflict, and on the other, on the weakness of the sense of individuality of the members of these communities. In some sense, by accepting to be reduced to a member of a well-defined identity group, they give up most of their identities. Communities subdue their members to such an extent that they seem to have lost their own individuality and personal experiences. In such a context, individuals cannot conceive of sharing a common truth with the members of other communities, and they save their own self-esteem disregarding diversity.

I.2

HUMAN RIGHTS IN IDENTITY-CONFLICTS:
THE MEANING OF 'HUMAN DIGNITY'

It is abundantly recognized that identity-conflicts entail increased levels of human rights abuses (Ignatieff 1997; Kaldor 1999, 2003a). The question here is to understand if it is possible to establish a causal link between increased levels of human rights violations and the escalation of violence. In other terms, do human rights' abuses trigger, or, at least, contribute to the emergence of these conflicts? According to a recent research carried out with the support of the Canadian International Development Agency's Human Rights and Participation Division, in order to answer to such a question it is necessary to distinguish two groups of rights: civil and political rights on the one hand, and economic, social and cultural rights on the other (Thoms and Ron 2007). The article shows that violations of both kinds of human rights are contributing factors of identity-conflicts. However, while massive violations of civil and political rights are more clearly recognizable as direct 'conflict triggers' (ibid.: 704), violations of the second set of rights are linked to conflicts in a sort of indirect way.

In the light of what has been stressed in the previous section, it is plausible to argue that violations and discriminations of political as well as socio-economic and cultural rights are underlying causes of conflict, fuelling social injustice and sectarian violence. In this perspective, human rights protection represents a fundamental moment in de-securitizing the conflict and a premise for the democratization process of divided societies. Very often, in these conflicts, the demand of human rights protection emerges from below, from the victims of abuses and discriminations. People perceive such violations as triggers and components of the conflict.[4] According to them, efforts in stopping such abuses and ensuring justice to the victims of human rights violations are needed to bring to an end the hostilities and build security. In the framework of this work, such a demand of human rights protection and justice for the victims of abuses functions as a core feature of people's 'culture of civility'. The associational bodies and structures of civil society are the *locus* where individuals articulate their experiences and express their demand of justice.

However, in deeply divided societies, two theoretical problems related to the idea of human rights are preliminarily to be faced. The first concerns their foundation and their extent, the second refers to their subjects.

1.2.1 The relative universality of human rights

What do we mean by human rights and what is their extent? Two extreme streams about 'rights' emerge from the Western philosophical tradition. One can define Hegelian historicism as that stream which sees culture, history and economics as the sources of all rights, while, a Kantian individualist stream would look at human rights as universal moral values, in no way subject to adaptation in the light of historical or cultural differences. Considered in their extreme versions, both views raise theoretical problems. Refusing the existence of any right out of a specific cultural and historical context, in some sense, the H-stream denies any universality of the idea of human rights. Conversely, breaking the link between rights and historical or cultural features the K-stream doctrine of rights becomes an *a priori* truth, a metaphysical doctrine theoretically implausible, and practically unacceptable for several societies.

It is therefore necessary to introduce a notion of human rights relatively independent from both streams, Kantian/universalism and Hegelian/historicism. The condition of protection of human rights in divided societies imposes upon us to rethink human rights as 'relative universal' values, in which cultural and historical features and universalistic acceptation of rights as fundamental values can converge (Donnelly 2007b).[5] Very often in conflict contexts, the quest of human rights protection emerges from below, from those who were victimized during the conflict. Frequently, they ignore the legal content of the rights they are appealing to; they just claim the protection and the recognition of their 'human dignity' as human beings.[6] The notion of human dignity entails a peculiar understanding of rights: namely, the rights one holds by virtue of being a person (Donnelly 1982, 1984, 2007b). Thus, at least prima facie, such a demand of human rights protection refers to an essential group of rights that are actually perceived by society as necessary to live a worthy life. In this perspective, human rights are universal since they are meant to be linked to the general condition of being human.

Conceptually, the notion of human dignity specifies the content of the human rights. Although, the idea of 'human dignity' finds a huge agreement in deeply different cultures and historical contexts, it would be misleading to treat these two notions — human rights and human dignity — as equivalent concepts (Donnelly 1982: 303). The claim of human dignity simply implies that human beings are equally 'worthy or deserving of respect' (Donnelly 2009: 10). Human rights reflect and seek to realize this particular sort of respect implied in the idea of human dignity. The global legal framework to protect human rights introduces a 'distinctive approach' or a distinctive institutional answer to the struggle for human dignity, based on a notion of equal concern and respect (see Donnelly 2003). In this view the idea of human dignity and its link to the contemporary universal notion of human rights is well synthesized in the first article of the UDHR:

> '*All human beings are born free and equal in dignity and rights*. They are endowed with reason and conscience and should act towards one another in a spirit of brotherhood' (UN 1948, emphasis added).

The emergence of an 'international legal universality' about human rights confirms that there is an emerging 'overlapping consensus' among different comprehensive religious or philosophical and moral doctrines on a 'political conception' based on the set human rights enumerated in the Universal Declaration of 1948.[7] The substantive conception of human rights of the Declaration gives the content and indicates the limits of political legitimacy in contemporary societies. This conception of human rights reflects those basic expectations that any human being may legitimately have of their societies and governments (Donnelly 2009: 7).

1.2.2 Group rights and human rights

The second issue introduces the collective versus individual rights debate, whether the moral subject of rights is an individual or a collective entity. Again, the deontological view of the 'right' is understood in opposition to a collective conception of the 'good'. At the root of this criticism is the communitarian criticism towards the liberal conception of a person as free and independent that introduces an idea of individuals as 'unencumbered by moral or civic ties they have not chosen' (Sandel 1982, 1996: 6). After a trip in former Yugoslavia in 1994, Ignatieff (1997: 6) wrote 'we in the West start from a universal ethic based on ideas of human rights, they start from particularistic ethics that define tribe, nation, and ethnicity as the limit of legitimate moral concern'.

Thus, the problem here concerns how to balance the competing and, sometimes, conflicting claims of individuals and communities. Is there any notion of group rights and, if so, should they be conceived as inherently collective or can they be reduced to the individual moral claims of its members?[8]

Once again, the debate can be developed around two extreme positions: a Kantian standpoint might suggest that all groups are reducible to its members, while a Hegelian perspective might be more prone to assume that a collective entity can have value independently of its members (Várady 1997; Jovanovich 2005). In this respect, Kymlicka (1996: 45; 2001) argues that such a debate is sterile 'because the question of whether the right is (or is not) collective is morally unimportant'. According to him, the moral issue concerns the demand of recognition: why do some groups in certain circumstances need to be differentiated with regard to their language, territory or religion? Since individual's identity and conscience are partly shaped by the recognition or by the misrecognition of others, the quest of recognition is the way in which individuals perceive themselves and their dignity through their *differentiation* (Taylor 1994). Therefore, his Liberal Multiculturalism represents an influential answer to the demand of cultural differentiation in contemporary democracies (Kymlicka 1996, 2001). As rightly pointed out by Parekh (2002), the root of Kymlicka's version of multiculturalism can be found in his notion of individual autonomy, according to which each individual should be free to develop his/her distinctive way of life. Here, the idea of culture is related to that of autonomy in a peculiar way: it informs individuals of the structures of their world and gives them a sense of identity (Kymlicka 1996). With respect to the first meaning, culture is therefore intimately related to contemporary democratic nation-states. For Kymlicka (2001), all contemporary democracies are based on a culturally defined idea of nation, where all citizens are supposed to share a distinct cultural identity. In this perspective, the contemporary notion of citizenship is deeply influenced by this culturally rooted idea of nation-state.

Understood in this way, contemporary democracies are necessarily prone to assimilate or exclude minorities and, thus, to un-dermine the autonomy of individuals who belong to these groups. In Kymlicka's view, these forms of assimilation or exclusion are prone to increase the inequalities within society, since minorities are often disadvantaged politically, socially and economically. In this perspective, the 'liberal rights to citizenship' does not satisfy the demand of social equality within society, since a liberal un-derstanding of rights overrides the relevance of the quest of differentiation of ethnic or minority groups (Kymlicka 1996: 45). In the face of this challenge, the idea of a 'multicultural citizenship' is aimed at incorporating a set of specific rights, namely minority rights, that should compensate the disadvantaged condition of these groups.

Thus, Kymlicka's argument in favour of multicultural citizenship is rooted in the assumption that in order to treat all citizens equally, a kind of differentiation based on the attribution of a specific set of rights — namely minority rights — is needed. However, it should be noted that the very idea of multicultural citizenship seems to refer to democratic systems where all individuals are recognized and recognize others as citizens. In this context, the distinction between ethnic/minority groups and the 'people', understood as national political community, is quite clear and all citizens, including those who are part of minority groups, belong to a consensus which makes them share and affirm the political conception of justice.

Actually, the absence of such a clear distinction between people and minority groups in deeply divided societies represents the crucial problem at stake. Again, the problem of the subject of minority rights becomes relevant. Indeed, if it is abundantly recognized as a collective right of 'peoples', rather than states or governments, to self-determination, with respect to minority rights it seems that both international law and political theory are likely to reduce the emphasis on the 'collective' dimension.[9] From a legal point of view in fact, the right to 'self-determination' enables 'people', understood as a social entity possessing a clear identity, to freely determine and pursue their political, economic and cultural interests and developments.[10] Conversely, with respect to minority rights, the General Assembly has recently clarified that:

> Governments should be sensitive towards *the rights of persons belonging to ethnic groups*, particularly their right to *lead lives of dignity*, to preserve their culture, to share equitably in the fruits of national growth and to play their part in the Government of the country of which they are citizens.[11] [Emphasis added]

Thus, it seems that in the case of minority rights the ultimate subjects are those 'individuals' who actually belong to specific ethnic, religious or cultural groups.

Conversely, the problem in divided societies is exactly that their members do not feel a part of a political community and ethnic minorities are often prone to see themselves as a distinct entity. They do not recognize former models of national sovereignty and, often, they ask their right to secession. In his latest works, Kymlicka himself has recognized that the success of Liberal Multiculturalism depends on three preconditions (e.g. geopolitical security, human rights guarantees and democratic accountability), which are absent in many war torn societies (Kymlicka 2007). He argues that 'in the absence of these conditions, models of multinational citizenship are unlikely to be adopted voluntarily, and if adopted under threat of violence or international pressure, are unlikely to have their intended "citizenizing" effects' (Kymlicka 2011: 328). Thus, the emphasis on the liberal ideal of autonomy of the minorities in these societies can be manipulated by political leaders in order to cultivate ethnic divisions and foster ethno-politics. Very often, the alleged minority groups are in fact inclined to define themselves in terms of 'people'.

These groups don't recognize themselves as members of a political community and ask their right to secede and to create their own national community. It is relevant to note in this respect that during and after an identity-conflict ethnic or religious minorities, rather than individuals, are targeted victims of abuses and violation (Vàrady 1997). A collective 'group', understood as a coherent unit, incorporates the subjects and societies appear deeply divided along ethnic or religious lines.

As for Bosnia, such an approach to minority rights led to a paradox: several political and civil rights are subjected to a declaration of belonging to one of three major ethnic groups.[12] It is important to consider that a moderate percentage (around 10 per cent of the population) of Jewish, Roma, Bulgarian, Albanian groups and mixed Bosnians are still living in Bosnia. Despite their Bosnian citizenship, most of the political and civil rights of these citizens are de-facto violated. This happens because these minor groups, defined as 'others', are excluded from ethno-representation.

To conclude, the problem of the identification of the subject of rights in deeply divided societies is not a sterile one, since it entails the possibility that a kind of 'ethnic citizenship' is adopted in violation of fundamental individuals' rights. As we have seen before, the problem of groups' agency may be modest if we look at it through the lens of the liberal autonomy of its members: thus group agency becomes plausible when the group is built on a voluntary basis and the freedom of exit for its members is guaranteed (Donnelly 2003). However, it is highly problematic when the group is ascribed and coercively defined and the violation of basic rights and freedoms of its members is perceived as necessary for the survival of the group itself.[13]

Again, the point of view of human dignity can be of some help: the recognition of cultural, ethnic or religious features is a process that starts from real individuals. Rather than 'unencumbered selves', individuals in plural societies have multiple ties and linkages but they share a 'sense of civility' towards each other rooted in a 'thin' notion of reciprocity and reasoned respect.

1.3

CIVIL SOCIETY, IDENTITY-CONFLICTS AND DEMOCRATIC TRANSITION:
THEORETICAL ISSUES

1.3.1 Democracy and pluralism in deeply divided societies

With reference to the idea of democratic transition, this work introduces several relevant issues. The first issue concerns the very idea democracy, and the actual possibility of enhancing democratic and pluralist values in deeply divided societies. As a matter of fact, the *praxis* of the last two decades has shown that the power of democratic states to intervene in such contexts and contain violence has decreased. The experience of recent 'humanitarian interventions' in Rwanda Somalia and ex-Yugoslavia, displays the failure of Western attempts to protect civilians, but, most importantly, these experiences have put into question the 'Western approach' to democratic transition, perceived by people as a top-down attempt to impose Western values and exercise a form of hegemonic power over the rest of the world. Analogous cases, experienced in Iraq and Afghanistan, and more recently in the north African region, have shown that democracy cannot be exported or imposed.[14] However, there are, at least, three theoretical problems linked to the idea of democracy in deeply divided societies. At the first level, there is a general relativistic scepticism towards the possibilities for democracy to be accepted in non-Western societies on the basis of a fundamental cultural difference between the West and the rest of the world. This kind of argument is rooted in the 'clash of civilizations' thesis (Huntington 1996). In this perspective, the recent wave of violence would suggest the decline of democracy as a universally recognized political value. As a part of the Western culture, democracy would entail rules and values which are unacceptable for other cultures and this will inevitably lead to a clash of civilizations (Huntington 1993).

At the second level, there is what I call the 'argument for toleration' at the global level; in this case scholars wonder whether we should conceive of democracy as a universal value. In his recent article 'Is there a Human Right to Democracy?', Joshua Cohen (2006) offers an interesting analysis, concluding that the 'conception of equality' linked to democracy entails an idea of justice too demanding for people who do not share that 'demanding political ideal'. In other words, if the acceptance of human rights standards is justified on the basis of a special 'urgency which transcends the urgency that surrounds considerations of justice generally' (ibid.: 233), this is not true for democracy that asks people to share the same 'demanding political ideal', which is implied in the principle of the equal right to participation. Cohen (2006: 20) says,

> democracy is not required as a matter of human rights: that too is true for us and them. A world with more democracy would be a more just world, because it gives people the treatment as equals to which all are entitled. But democracy, with its equal right to participate, is not part of the common standard of achievement, defensible on the terrain of global public reason, to which global public responsibility extends.

Finally at the third level, the main problem is how it is possible to reconcile the condition of a normative consensus with the sort of pluralism that characterizes deeply divided societies. A fundamental problem in contemporary democratic theory is related to the combination of two fundamental political ideas: pluralism and consensus (Dryzeck and Niemeyer 2006).

Notably, John Rawls's solution to this dilemma is based on two related ideas, the idea of 'overlapping consensus' and the idea of public reason (Rawls 2005). For him, 'the fact of pluralism' alone cannot ensure that all citizens will affirm the same 'political conception' (ibid.: 180). In this sense, a well ordered democratic society is unified and stable if there is an overlapping consensus among different comprehensive doctrines which supports the political conception (ibid.: 133). In other terms, an overlapping consensus occurs when political liberalism as a meta-theory is affirmed by citizens with different but reasonable moral views.[15]

The notion of overlapping consensus is deeply related to an idea of liberal legitimacy (ibid.: 134–40). This is because the political conception entails two relevant features: it is aimed at regulating the relationships among individuals within the basic structure and the kind of political power is always a coercive power (ibid.: 135–36). But, if political authority is always coercive and should regulate a basic structure in which citizens have different comprehensive doctrines, the only political power acceptable and possible is that which is in accordance with principles which could be reasonably accepted and endorsed by any member of a plural society (ibid.: 136). In this sense, the principle of political legitimacy is related to that of moral stability in a plural society. An overlapping consensus is therefore not a mere balance of powers; it implies a form of stability for the 'right reasons' because all citizens agree on one political conception, the liberal one, for different moral reasons which derive from their different comprehensive doctrines.

A second relevant feature, linked to the idea of moral pluralism and its inclusion in the democratic processes, is Rawls's idea of public reason. This notion is part of Rawls's constitutional design, in the sense that it imposes the limits to the public deliberation over fundamental constitutional issues in a plural democratic society. It applies to specific issues, namely those issues which are part of the 'public political forum', with specific characteristics, binding for all, and it is directed to a specific group of people, which includes judges, politicians government officials.[16] The idea of public reason is linked to both reciprocity and political legitimacy. On the one hand, the criterion of reciprocity defines the terms under which public reason should be formulated in a way that others can reasonably accept and understand. On the other, the idea of liberal legitimacy is related to that of 'duty of civility', which is a moral duty of all citizens to provide reciprocally reasonable explanations for their political actions.

However, can this form of 'normative consensus', based on ideas such as reasonable pluralism and democratic legitimacy, be useful to consider the case of transitional societies? As we know, Rawls refers to the case of a 'well ordered' society; how then can we achieve some sort of 'stability for the right reasons' in societies where clashes of identities and the memory of past atrocities deeply undermine the sense of citizenship?

If the general relativistic scepticism of the first critique is easily falsified if we take seriously democracy as a political conception rather than a metaphysical doctrine, the second and the third issues pose serious theoretical challenge to conceive of democracy in deeply divided societies. In the next two sections, I first defend an ideal of democracy based on a general practice of 'giving reasons' which is shared in many different societies. In this sense, it would be possible to at least conceive of democracy as a universal value or ideal. I will then introduce the argument based on the idea of 'culture of civility'. In divided societies the fact of pluralism can hardly be framed into a framework of reasonableness. However, a kind of agreement is still possible. This is what I call the culture of civility, which can be understood as a kind of non-institutional consensus on a specific tradition of civility, made up of shared values and traditions, which enables individuals to become part of a community of citizens and accept to reciprocate on the basis of some universal values, such as condemnation of racist regimes or respect of human dignity. In essence, the idea of a culture of civility aims at addressing both justice and a kind of stability for the 'right reasons' in the process of transition of divided societies.

1.3.2 Democracy as a universal ideal

The political scientist Robert Dahl has recognized two dimensions of democracy (Dahl 2000). The first dimension concerns its ideal representation: democracy is therefore conceived as an ideal, a goal, an unachievable standard.

The second dimension, then, is more connected to the practices and the actual rules and procedures of contemporary democracies. However, it would be misleading to ignore the first dimension in favour of the second one. This would underrate the relevance of the intimate link existing between people and their ideal of democracy.

The relevance of the first dimension of democracy becomes even more evident in deeply divided societies where citizens experience a deep detachment from democratic institutions. In the literature on conflict transformation, the issue of democracy building in divided societies is represented as a crucial one. In a recent book, Roland Paris has suggested a new peace-building strategy called 'Institutionalization before Liberalization' (Paris 2004), emphasizing the relevance of the phase of 'institution-building'. According to him, a controlled and gradual approach to democratization is needed in the first post-conflict period. Such an approach is supposed to create the governmental structures and institutions needed to sustain further political and economic reforms. However, if it is true that strong and accountable institutions are at the core of any democratic system, nonetheless it is extremely dangerous to consider the possibility of imposing these institutions on a community. Let us consider the case of a constitution. Such a legal instrument undoubtedly represents a crucial institutional device; without a constitution, the democratic system is not even conceivable. However, if a domestic constitution is imposed through an external effort on an emerging political community, it is unable to create the sort of moral stability required for a democratic society alone. In Bosnia, for example, in the framework of the Dayton Agreement a democratic constitution has been imposed on Bosnian citizens. Nevertheless, after more than 15 years such an effort has not led to a viable and actual democratic system in the country. All these observations show the limits of Paris's approach. Overriding the relevance of the first dimension of democracy, such an approach is likely to be ineffective. Furthermore, it is more prone to emphasize the detachment of people from politics that characterizes deeply divided societies.

Conversely, thinking of democracy as a fundamental political ideal may be of some help in this context. Such an understanding has received too little recognition both in theory and in practice until now.[17] Democracy is much more than political elections and multiparty competition, these elements constitute only one part of a broader picture. The idea of democracy in its first acceptation may help to respond to the challenge raised by the 'argument for toleration' discussed in the previous section, since a first kind of this 'ideal' can be found in those practices of public reasoning and of liberal tolerance familiar to many different traditions. As Amartya Sen has argued, in this broad sense there is a long democratic tradition in several non-western societies that should be taken seriously into account by western scholars.[18] Thus, an inclusive idea of democracy can be built starting from 'the dialogic part of the common human inheritance'.

What we need in post-conflict divided societies is to emphasize the common 'sense of civility' already existing in the society. An effective approach to democratic transition has therefore to start from below and has to take into account the cultural specificity and the sense of civility emerging from those people who are actually involved in the democratization process. In those contexts, the ideal and universal value of democracy is deeply linked to the preservation of human dignity and the restoration of a pluralistic dialogue based on thin forms of public reasoning and tolerance.

1.3.3 Civil society as the sphere for non-institutional consensus: the idea of culture of civility

The second issue concerns the link between democracy, intended in such a broad sense, and civil society. In the last section, the relevant role of people in producing their own quest of democracy has been emphasized. This means that the democratization process has to start from below, from societies. Nevertheless, very often the involvement of societies can be ambivalent and controversial. For this reason, it is important to have a normative idea of civil society, in which the idea of 'civility' represents the link existing among people involved in society and the ideal of democracy.

In this book, civil society is the sphere placed among the three spheres of politics, culture and economy. Of course, such an idea of civil society is not aimed at emphasizing those features of democracy already present at the societal level. The assumption that civil society, as such, can be used in the place of democracy is, at least, questionable. Furthermore, it is extremely difficult to conceive of democracy as independent from a system of fair institutions. However, it seems possible to refer to an idea of civil society as that sphere, between 'family and state', where some of those universal values that constitute the 'public political culture' (Rawls 2005) of a liberal democracy may emerge in the form of a 'common culture of civility'.

It is true that democratic institutions are necessary to sustain an inclusive and democratic civil society. Yet, as Walzer (2003: 79) argues 'the civility that makes democratic politics possible can only be learned in the associational networks' which populate the sphere of civil society. In literature, it is possible to find a huge agreement about the intimate link between civil society and democracy. Since ancient times, the debate about civil society has been built around a fundamental political issue concerning the role of freedom in the political realm (Cohen and Arato 1994). Whatever has been the approach to society, the relations between public and private as well as between public ethics and individual interest have represented key features of modern political thought. Accordingly, it is possible to distinguish two broad versions of civil society's understandings. On one side, following Tocqueville, an idea of civil society as a tool of stabilization of democratic regimes has emerged. This version highlights the fundamental link existing between the associational and voluntary sector and the democratic functioning of contemporary states. According to this view, civil society can be seen as a democratic expedient in a specific way. It is able to modify or, at least, correct the democratic direction of politics through the formation of 'public opinion' (Habermas 1989, 1996). On the other hand, starting from the Hegelian idea of the ethical content of civil society as distinct from the state, an idea of civil society of an anti-political kind has been developed. This perspective introduces a counter-hegemonic dimension for civil society. Civil society is considered as a means of rebellion or, at least, contestation against the state.

Starting from these two versions, contemporary scholars have developed different approaches to civil society. They combine such versions with the three dimensions of civil society, offering three different readings of civil society: namely, cultural, economic and political approaches to civil society.

(1) The first approach is the 'post-colonial' version of civil society (see also Kaldor 2002, 2003a, 2003b). According to post-colonial scholars, the idea of civil society can be reframed in the light of the possibilities for a cultural counter-hegemony, a counterweight to the imperialistic hegemony of the West. Such an approach, in fact, emphasizes the limits of a Western-oriented notion of civil society. The core idea relies on considering the existence of traditional groups and organizations, based on religion, ethnicity, or kinship, as an alternative public space (Comaroff and Comaroff 1999). Instead of the notions of voluntarism and autonomy, the post-colonial version of civil society recovers the ascriptive criteria of kinship or religion, producing a combination of communitarian-corporatism and libertarianism (Zubaida 2001; Obadare 2004).

(2) According to the second approach, the 'neo-liberal' version (see Kaldor 2002, 2003a, 2003b), civil society is seen as an economic actor, the Third Sector. In this perspective, a strong voluntary and autonomous non-profit sector, namely the third sector, produces comparative advantages for both market and state. On the one hand, such an idea is linked to the neo-liberal perspective of minimizing the role of the state in order to have more efficiency in the market. On the other, this approach emphasizes Tocqueville's idea of the fundamental link

between the existence of a strong associational and voluntary sector and the democratic functioning of contemporary states (Putnam 1995; Fukuyama 1999).

(3) Finally, a 'cosmopolitan' civil society has recently been developed. It combines features of political philosophy with international relations theories. In this third understanding, the new idea of civil society is linked to the political sphere. According to cosmopolitan scholars, in a context in which nation-states do not any longer have the authority to defend their citizens, new civil society movements and organizations represent a sort of interface between the individuals and the state (Kaldor 2003b). They emphasize the emancipatory potential of such a global dimension of civil society. Global civil society provides the framework within which the resistance of individuals against both authoritarianism and global market can be mobilized (Cox 2003).

An examination of the three contemporary approaches shows two kinds of problems, in some way connected to each other. First, each approach of civil society focuses on one of the two versions: civil society as a means of stabilization, and civil society as a means of contestation. However, on the one hand, civil society as a means of stabilization would require democracy and a strong state as prior conditions. As argued by Foley and Edwards (1996: 40), autonomous civic groups can also include that un-democratic and conflicting side of society, which 'in absence of political settlements and rules may spill over into disruption and violence'. On the other hand, emphasizing the emancipatory potential of civil society as a 'counterweight' to the state implies that this anti-political potential could be a challenge for a democratic as well as for an authoritarian state (Foley and Edwards 1996).

The problem here is that, even if from opposite sides, these two approaches present the same circularity: they depend on democratic structures. Of course, both the ideas of stabilization and contestation represent important features in civil society discourses; but they cannot guarantee a role for civil society independent from democratic rules and procedures. It follows that none of these approaches can be applied in situations of a collapsed state and of deeply divided societies. A normative notion of civil society may instead reproduce that intimate link between people and the ideal of democracy, which makes it 'civil' even out of a democratic context.

Second, such a circularity depends on the fact that contemporary approaches fail in grasping the central argument of civil society, which concerns the balance among the three dimensions of economy, politics and culture.

Civil society, as proposed in the present work, intends to be a liberal reading of Hegelian civil society. I recover from Hegelian philosophy some features that I take as necessary for conceiving of civil society as an intermediate dimension between family and state. In such a context, civil society is conceived as a bearer of specific cultural and historical developments, and of rights and values. Furthermore, the liberal account makes this framework individual-oriented, rather than collective-oriented, since it looks at the system of needs as the primary source of civil society.

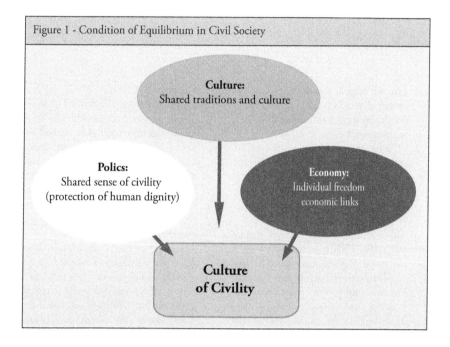

Figure 1 - Condition of Equilibrium in Civil Society

Culture:
Shared traditions and culture

Polics:
Shared sense of civility
(protection of human dignity)

Economy:
Individual freedom
economic links

**Culture
of Civility**

NOTES

1. I am referring here to the economic approach of 'greed vs grievances' and to the political approach to 'new nationalism'; see chapters 2.
2. "The freedom to determine our loyalties and priorities between the different groups to all of which we may belong is a peculiarly important liberty which we have reason to recognize, value and defend" (Sen 2006a: 5).
3. This is also supported by several empirical studies. Collier and the supporters of the 'greed vs grievances approach' have empirically shown that in many cases of identity-conflicts there is an inverse link between multiethnicity and violence. According to them, the relevant factor in fuelling violence would be rather represented by the existence of one strong ethnic group. The presence of such empirical studies is deeply rooted in the assumption that particular interests rather than collective claims would be underlying features of these conflicts. Of course, this assumption cannot be considered as a clear rule, since there are cases where the multiethnic character of society represents a factor of deep instability – as in the case of Bosnia (Collier and Hoeffler 2004)
4. With regard to citizens' perceptions of human rights violations, see also (Carlson and Listhaug 2007).
5. Elsewhere, Donnelly (2003: 98) has rightly argued that 'We do not face an either-or choice between cultural relativism and universal rights. Rather, we need to recognize both the universality of human rights and their particularity and thus accept a certain limited relativity.'
6. See, for instance, chapter 4 for the meaning of human dignity and justice as perceived by Bosnian associations of victims and relatives of missing persons.
7. According to Rawls, the idea of overlapping consensus, as a way to balance stability and pluralism, is the result of a process of human and moral development and he shows how an 'initial acquiescence in a liberal conception of justice as a mere modus vivendi could change over time first into a constitutional consensus and then into an overlapping consensus' (Rawls 2005: 168). Therefore, as Maffettone (2010) rightly points out, the moral stability of such an overlapping consensus is also supported by a notion of the sense of justice, which is not so different from the idea expressed in the third part of the Theory of Justice. Again, the idea of a sense of justice deriving from having grown up under just institutions turns out to be a crucial element in rendering them stable even in a society with a plurality of comprehensive doctrines.

8. On this debate, see also Donnelly (2003: 204–20).

9. 'All peoples have the right of self-determination. By virtue of that right, they freely determine their political status and freely pursue their economic, social, and cultural development', Articles 1 of both covenants, see OHCHR (1976a, 1976b).

10. 'The two important United Nations studies on the right to self-determination set out factors of a people that give rise to possession of right to self-determination: a history of independence or self-rule in an identifiable territory, a distinct culture, and a will and capability to regain self-governance' (Parker 2000).

11. See OHCHR (1996). General Recommendation No. 21: Right to self-determination: 23/08/1996. Gen. Rec. No. 21. (General Comments), paragraph 5.

12. The right to be elected, to work in the public administration, etc.

13. A difference can be made with reference to the case of indigenous people. However, one should note that in this as well as in other cases of reconciliation between indigenous people and national majorities, the politics of reconciliation needs to include a kind of recognition of an original right to self-determination, understood as a form of 'non interference'. This right could be justified not only as a form of reparation for past abuses and protection from future challenges to both integrity and autonomy of these groups, but also as a necessary condition in order to protect their same existence. This kind of interpretation can be also sustained from a legal perspective, due to the recent developments in International Law. In the UN Declaration on Rights of Indigenous People of 2007, the distinction between minority groups/people and collectives vs individuals becomes less evident. Indigenous peoples are considered both as a collective and as a group of individuals. In addition, the declaration recognizes a kind of self-determination which is hardly recognizable for other kinds of national minorities. Indigenous people are defined as 'distinctive peoples' and their right to self-determination includes a protection of their cultural traditions and their integrity as people and the recognition of a special link between these peoples and their lands. Therefore, from a theoretical point of view, indigenous right to self-determination can be defended as a way to ensure their existence and does not affect the sovereign authority of the state.

14. A vast literature has emerged on this subject in the last years (Diamond 2005; Enterline and Michael 2008; Kinsman 2011; Sakbani 2011).

15. On this interpretation of Political Liberalism as both a comprehensive doctrine and a 'meta-theory', see also Maffettone (2010: 215).

16. According to many scholars, however, the inclusion of ordinary citizens in this group is instead controversial. In this respect, Rawls says that citizens should act according to the ideal of the public reason when they vote, but he leaves great space for citizens to express their own views. On this point see Maffettone (2010).

17. I refer, for instance, to the case of post-intervention Iraq, in the attempt to get straight to polling, peace-builders and theorists have shown too little interest in fostering a public political culture and supporting an independent civil society.

18. I am here referring to an article that appeared in *The Economist* in March 2006, titled 'Democracy isn't "Western"' (Sen 2006b).

Chapter 2

At the root of deeply divided societies: understanding ethno-religious conflicts

2.1 Post-modern conflicts: disappearance of Clausewitzean warfare – 2. 2 Conflicts over identity claims: exploring the meaning of identity in conflict – 2.3 Identity in conflict: lack of freedoms and the limits of rationality

Societies may be divided in several different ways and the kind of cleavages emerging in these contexts often have important political salience. However, if it is true that contemporary societies are crossed by several divisions, only in a few cases are these cleavages able to produce deep divisions within societies. It is therefore necessary to define 'deeply divided societies' as a specific category and distinguish these societies from other plural societies.[1] In this book, I refer in particular to the case of societies that are torn by violent ethno-religious conflicts. Since the end of the Cold War, ethno-religious conflicts have been the main cause of humanitarian catastrophes and a major threat to both local and international peace and stability (Kaldor 1999; Kymlicka 2007). As a consequence of these tensions, deep divisions along ethnic and religious lines have increasingly emerged in several regions of the world. After years of ethnic or religious violence and atrocities in societies like Bosnia or Rwanda people do not recognize themselves as members of a political community, and identity politics is pursued, often in violent forms, at the expense of liberal democratic projects and reconciliation programmes (Dryzek 2005).

This chapter offers an analysis of ethno-religious conflicts and their impact on the polarization that is a common feature in divided societies. Therefore, in the general framework of the present book 'ethno-religious conflicts' represent the context of the analysis. Normative political philosophers tend to look at the is-sue of the 'context' in a sceptical way. For them, too much emphasis on contexts would reduce the generality and universality of the theory. Conversely, anthropologists, sociologists and political scientists are inclined to give a certain priority to the context, to the particular over the general. In the present book,

I offer a third view about the role of the context. Even though the contextual-ization of the theory is likely to reduce its universal applicability, it seems nec-essary to understand the specific case of deeply divided societies in the light of an analysis of the causes that are at the root of the polarization. In addition, the analysis of ethno-religious conflicts is understood here as a part of the general theory; awareness about the meaning of identity, nation/nationalism, and *group-ness* represents the first theoretical challenge in order to discuss the possibilities for democratic transition in these societies. The recent episodes of interventions in situations of ethno-religious conflicts, have shown that a deep awareness about the meaning and impact of such theoretical issues is crucial in order to offer ap-propriate answers.[2]

   This chapter presents the following structure: The first section offers an in-troduction to the ethno-religious conflicts and their impact on international com-munity. I discuss the difficulty in looking at such conflicts through the lenses of the classic Clausewitzean theory, and the recent approaches that have emerged in international relations, security studies and political economy. In the last two decades, two opposite ways to describe and understand violence have been de-veloped. I call these two views culturalist and rational choice perspectives. (1) On the one hand, a culturalist approach, based on the idea of an unavoidable clash of 'civilizations', has been developed (Huntington 1993; Kaplan 1993; Huntington 1996). According to this view, the end of the balance of powers, guaranteed by the 'system' of the Cold War, has made room for the emergence of ancient cul-tural and religious rivalries among and within nations (Kaplan 1993; Luttwak 1995). This approach sees such rivalries in a primordial perspective; the clash of civilizations represents an underlying challenge for Western culture, and there is no way to face it through the traditional democratic means. Since democracy repre-sents a peculiar aspect of 'Western civilization', democratic means are questioned because they are inapplicable to other 'civilizations', given that they are part of Western culture. (2) On the other hand, the rational choice approach empha-sizes the peculiarity of such new forms of violence and links this new reality to the emergence of a globalized post-national system. Violence would be the re-action to new imbalances in global and domestic economies, to market changes in the availability of weapons, and, what seems more important, to the erosion of nation-state attributions and power, which made room for new sectarian iden-tities able to undermine the sense of shared political community (Kaldor 1999, 2003b, 2004, 2005). Most of these theorists consider these conflicts as 'new forms of violence' that require 'new' cosmopolitan answers for Western liberalism.

   According to my view, both approaches fail in grasping the true essence of these conflicts. Even if it is true that the globalization processes emphasize the extent and the impact of such conflicts, it would be misleading to believe that there is a link between increased levels of ethnic or religious violence and globalization. Several empirical studies demonstrate that the level of violence and the impact on the civilians has decreased since the end of the Cold War, even if with an irregular trend (Kalyvas 2001; Eriksson et al. 2003; Melander et al. 2009). This counter-globalization argument is also argued from a theoretical point of view. Actually, several scholars maintain that in most of the less developed countries the dynamics of nation-state making, rather than globalization processes, are supposed to ignite violent internal conflicts (Ayoob 1996; Min et al. 2007). These considerations suggest the significance of paying more attention to the peculiar factor of these conflicts that concerns the identity–violence nexus.

The second section is devoted to a brief analysis of the main authors who started exploring the complex interconnections between culture and violence. Galtung, Azar and contemporary theorists highlight the urgency of paying attention to such a link. In this section, following Amartya Sen, I investigate the meaning of identity seen as the sum of a variety of plural affiliations. Culturalist and rational choice supporters suggest two extreme ways to look at identity in conflict: a cultural reductionism derives from the primordialist perspective suggested by the first group of scholars, while an individualist reductionism emerges from the constructivist account proposed by both versions of rational choice theory. The idea of multiple identities shows the limits of both reductionisms offering a third way to look at the identity issue in conflict. Nevertheless, if it is true that individual identity can be described as the sum of a plurality of affiliations, the preliminary issue to be solved concerns the evidence of several internal conflicts, which seems to suggest that, given specific conditions, some affiliations, namely ethnicity, religion or ethno-language, tend to overcome the others. I explain such a phenomenon in the light of a deeper understanding of the idea of nation. I discuss the historical and theoretical reasons that produced an understanding of the ideas of nation and territory as culturally rooted.

In the last section, I develop an approach to ethno-religious conflicts that takes into serious account the idea of multiple identities. This section is split into two different parts. A first *pars destruens*, where I criticize the two reductionisms testing the empirical assumption to an actual conflict-case (the Bosnian war 1992–95), is followed by the *construens* section, where I articulate an analysis of identity-conflicts that, even accepting an individualistic-rooted understanding of violence, does not underrate the role played by identity-based claims.

(1) On one hand, by readapting Azar's PSC theory to contemporary identity-conflicts it is possible to focus the attention on the basic-needs deprivation at the root of violence. Such a perspective suggests that the condition of capa-

bility-deprivation, understood as a lack of basic political rights and freedoms, economic opportunities and cultural recognition and free expression, generates widespread grievances and frustrations within society, which are the preconditions for violent identity-conflicts.

(2) On the other hand, it is necessary to pay attention to those private forms of violence that emerge in contexts of conflict. Very often, master cleavages, based on ethno-religious arguments, represent tools that are employed by private – sometimes criminal – individuals or associations, which I call 'cultural-war-entrepreneurs', in order to create a certain level of support to their violent actions. The impact of such actors in conflict can be explained as an odd combination of two distinct ideas of war: a Hobbesian perspective of private war – *homo homini lupus* – and a Rousseauian conception of public interest. Accordingly, private interests overcome and manipulate collective claims. In the long term, such actors create new local powers based on what Foucault would have called 'bio-power', based on race/ethno- or religious supremacy, able to protract the condition of war in situations of 'presumed peace'. This perspective reverses the Clausewitzean understanding of war, since it introduces Foucault's idea that in such deeply divided societies the so-called 'peace' is a 'continuation of war by other means'. The case of Bosnia is illustrative of how such a process of 'continuation of war by other means' works in a deeply divided society.

2.1
POST-MODERN CONFLICTS:
DISAPPEARANCE OF CLAUSEWITZEAN WARFARE

In the last two decades, scholars from different fields have paid growing attention to the search for new paradigms and explanations to apply to wars, with a special attention to internal conflicts. According to them, the post–Cold War era has seen the emergence of new kinds of conflicts that have questioned the traditional Clausewitzean understanding of war.

War, in Clausewitz's thought, is mainly a social phenomenon, and, like any other social phenomenon, involves a conflict of interests and a series of activities. Clausewitz's description of war, as a continuation of politics by other means, is quite instructive in such a sense. The distinction between peace and war is significantly represented by the intervention of violence. According to him, if it becomes impossible to achieve political objectives through peaceful means, then the war occurs as a precise 'act of violence to compel the enemy to fulfill our will'.[3] In such a framework, the idea of war is deeply rooted in the modern understanding of state. The development of the modern nation-states, based on a specific territorial space and controlled by centralized and rational structures, is an achievement that can be traced back to the end of the nineteenth century. Such an attainment is the outcome of a historical process that encompasses almost a century of struggles, from the French Revolution to the emergence of the last European nations, Italy and Germany in the late nineteenth century. The introduction of state armies based on compulsory conscription guaranteed the monopoly of the legitimate violence.

According to several scholars, the end of the Cold War and the emergence of a globalized system have deeply challenged the modern understanding of war and peace. Since the content of the modern nation-state cannot represent a valid paradigm any more, it follows that with reference to wars also we should find new paradigms able to grasp the shifts of the current age (Kaldor 1999). Market globalization, on the one hand, and the disappearance of the Soviet Union on the other, produced a deep shift in world politics, which has deeply questioned the authority and legitimacy of the nation-state model. According to Beck (2002), it is difficult, but not impossible, to understand the contemporary human condition nationally or locally. For Habermas (2001) the market pressure has irremediably undermined the social, fiscal and political basis of the modern nation-state. In other terms, the policies of economic globalization require the dismantling of state institutions (Anheier and Isar 2007) and weakened states cannot provide equal protection for their citizens. Furthermore, the image of the world as a global village had a huge effect on the migration flows, which consistently increased in the last two decades (see also OECD-ORG 2007). The impact of such migration flows on the industrialized societies has been dramatic, turning homogeneous nations into heterogeneous societies, and introducing vast differences in wealth, values and cultural practices (Crawford 2007).

In addition to this, the disappearance of the 'second super-power', the Soviet Union, has intervened as a further factor of instability at both local and global levels. At the global level, the end of the Cold War marked the beginning of a new political era characterized by the nonlinear alternation of two different approaches to global politics: an imperfect American unilateralism on one side, and a more responsive, even if sometimes less effective, multilateralism, on the other. The interventions in Afghanistan and Iraq, on the one hand, and in Bosnia and Rwanda, on the other, represent clear examples of the application of these two approaches in concrete contexts of war. At the local level, then, the decline of the Soviet Union made room for the explosion of violent local clashes for the self-determination of new national entities. Western countries had to cope with huge flows of displaced persons, refugees, Diaspora groups, but also criminal groups and local mafias, coming from failing countries.

One can summarize at least three main factors that have brought new attention to the ethno-religious conflicts and their role in the international arena:

i   Possibilities of intervention: since the risk of escalation into a full-scale world war ceased to exist; the military or political intervention in local conflicts — which affected less-developed countries all over the world — has become a concrete option for Western societies (Wimmer et al. 2004).

ii Reasons for the intervention: with the disappearance of the Soviet system, Western political and economic doctrines seemed to be almost globally valid. However, two contrasting attitudes emerged in Western societies. On the one hand, Western governments seemed to feel a sense of responsibility/duty towards less developed countries, and therefore towards their achievements in terms of stable peace, democracy, good governance and human rights protection. In this perspective, the interventions in ethno-religious conflicts became a 'testing ground for a new morality of promoting peace, stability, and human rights across the globe' (Wimmer et al. 2004b: 1). On the other hand, the new market pressure towards an even more global system imposed on Western countries the necessity to intervene in local conflicts in order to guarantee the development of foreign investments and economic stability in those failed countries.

iii New security agenda: the ethno-religious wars, especially in the Balkans, Iraq, Sri Lanka and Ethiopia, produced huge flows of refugees, immigrants and Diaspora groups. If this phenomenon enhances awareness of living in a unified global system, it nevertheless triggers new delocalized struggles and violence. Furthermore, many Western governments considered such small-scale conflicts in newly independent states of the East or in democratizing states in the South as the underlying threat to global peace and stability.

In the light of the previous observations, the approach to 'new wars' seems to offer a view about the entire reality of the post–Cold War era. Scholars from different perspectives offer two general approaches to new wars. Although they agree that contemporary forms of violence and conflict are peculiar of the current age and that there is an intimate link between such new wars and the phenomenon of globalization, these authors offer two different explanatory paradigms for these post-modern conflicts and two opposite answers in terms of global politics. In order to clarify the perspectives offered by these two schools of theorists, I distinguish two approaches: culturalism and rational choice theory applied to conflicts.[4] In the following sections, I outline the main features and limits of the two approaches and I offer a third view about ethno-religious conflicts more related to the identity–violence nexus.

Table 1 - 'New Wars'		
	CULTURALIST PERSPECTIVE → PRIMORDIALISM → POST-STATISM	RATIONAL CHOICE THEORY → CONSTRUCTIVISM → COSMOPO-LITANISM
External Causes	Globalisation / Erosion of the nation-state attributions	Globalisation / Erosion of the nation-state attributions
Internal Causes	Ancient hatred based on ethnic religious features	Economic (Greed) or political private interests
Impact of Violence	Local and Global	Local and Global
Targeted Victims	Other cultural groups (civilizations)	Civilians & Non-combatants

2.1.1 Culturalist perspective and post-statism

The idea of 'new wars' proposed by culturalist scholars generally entails a post-statist perspective. It is based on two primary assumptions: the end of the Cold War and the emergence of a globalized system, and the reappearance of ancient ethnic and cultural hatreds (Huntington 1993, 1996).

(1) The first argument is eminently political. The traditional statist approach was based on four key assumptions:

a)   the state is the most important actor in international relations,
b)   the state is a unitary and rational actor,
c)   international relations are essentially conflicting because of anarchy, which means that a bipolar system of balance of powers is more effective than a multipolar distribution of power,
d)   security and strategic issues, known as high politics, dominate the international agenda. The collapse of the Soviet Union and the emergence of a new phenomenon, known as globalization, deeply questioned the validity of such assumptions.

According to these authors, if the theory — and the practice — of deterrence, ensured by the balance of power, influenced aligned and non-aligned nations to avoid international and sometimes internal violence, the disappearance of a 'culture of disciplined constraints on the use of the force' (Luttwak 1995: 110) caused, as consequence, the explosion of violent identity-conflicts in several regions of the world.

(2) The second assumption introduces the cultural dimension. The main idea is that due to the disappearance of many authoritarian regimes, preserved by the balance of powers, 'ancient hatreds' marked along ethnic and cultural lines are being revived and increased by conflicting claims to self-determination and political sovereignty (Kaplan 1993, Callahan 1998). In this sense, this view is primordialist and strongly essentialist: ethnic and religious divisions have always existed and are only now erupting because the Cold War's end has loosed the imperial hands that kept them down.

Undoubtedly, Huntington's clash of civilizations vastly influenced such an understanding of conflicts. In his view, civilizations are the most dangerous challenge for nation-states in the current age. Civilizations are supposed to be the 'highest cultural grouping of people and the broadest level of cultural identity people have' (Huntington 1993: 24). He identifies eight major cultural groups differentiated from each other by language, culture and religion.[5] Thus, 'clashes of civilizations are the greatest threat to world peace' and 'in the post Cold War world the most important distinctions among people are not ideological, political, or economic, they are cultural' (Huntington 1996: 321). The 'fault lines between civilizations' have emerged in Europe replacing the political and ideological boundaries of the Cold War and these boundaries of 'cultural differences' are likely to become lines of bloody conflicts (Huntington 1993: 29).

The argument for civilizations is inherently relativistic and introduces a strong scepticism towards the possibilities for dialogue and cooperation among different cultural groups. Either liberal or neo-liberal approaches cannot succeed in dealing with non-Western civilizations, because neither democracy as both institutional model and moral value, nor neo-liberal market economy can be fully accepted out of the West (Huntington 1993: 39–41). Western efforts in spreading such values have, in fact, the effect to revive strong reactions against 'human rights imperialism' (Huntington 1993: 41) and to enhance sectarian and identitarian violence. If a possibility to face such 'new clashes of civilizations' and to coexist with the other civilizations does exist, it cannot be represented by democracy and Western values. According to the author, the future security agenda will be marked by an existential unavoidable struggle between 'us', the West, and the other civilizations, 'the rest'. In addition, Kaplan criticizes Western attempts to plant democracy abroad, in contexts in where 'it cannot succeed' (Kaplan 2000). For him, the destabilizing role played by democracy and democratic values in postcolonial states is creating what he calls 'the coming anarchy', and he stresses the urgency to restore a realist approach to international politics replacing the idealist perspective based on ideas such as cosmopolitan democracy (Kaplan 1997, 2000).

2.1.2 Rational choice theory and cosmopolitan answer

The second approach to new wars can be understood as liberal defence of democracy and Western political institutions and values from the challenge of cultural relativism imposed by culturalist post-statist perspective.

This approach shares with the previous one the idea that the phenomenon of the new wars is linked to the emergence of a globalized system that encompasses not only market economy but also political and cultural values. However, there are at least three key features of 'new wars' which differentiate this approach from the previous one:

a) New actors: warlords, Diaspora groups, child soldiers, paramilitary groups, private companies play a significant role in such conflicts. This phenomenon has serious consequences in terms of dissolving centres of power, complexity of relations, shifting alliances, and, furthermore, it emphasizes the inadequacy of traditional nation-state structures to face new forms of violence (Duffield 1998, Collier & Hoeffler 2004, Fearon 2005).

(b) Use/misuse of identity claims: the identity-based character of such conflicts 'has to be understood as socially constructed responses to globalization' (Kaldor 2004, Bellamy 2002: 34); it represents the key instrument for the new actors in order to secure support and legitimacy from the population even though living standards may be falling.

(c) New forms of violence: The new forms of violence are spectacular since the targets are global, instead of local, therefore 'suicide attacks' as well as other forms of violence are designed for maximum media impact (Kaldor 2004). This 'new barbarism' (Bellamy 2002: 25) emerged in such conflicts represents also an instrument that new actors use to ensure loyalty. In Bosnia, for example, Serb leaders made the war as brutal as possible in order to ensure the loyalty of the Bosnian Serb population, in this context the violence is a way to 'establish new friend-enemy distinctions' (Kaldor 2005: 42). Most importantly, new violence is targeted against 'civilians' or 'non-combatants'.

The most important difference between these two approaches relies however on the anti-essentialist character of this second view and its criticism of the argument of 'ancient hatreds'. If it is true that new sectarian identities based on ethnic or religious features emerge in new wars: these identities are 'constructed' rather than 'given'. The primordial perspective is therefore not only inadequate to explain the sectarian violence of new conflicts, but also it provides us with a dangerous relativistic argument, 'those who perceive war as based on ancient rivalries and support war for that purpose are the more extreme nationalist and religious fundamentalist groups' (Kaldor 2007: 101). For this approach, thus, ethnic and religious divisions are 'deliberately fostered for the purpose of winning power' (ibid.: 104).

It is possible to identify at least two sets of emerging literatures that challenge the canons of the 'ancient hatred' approach. These two views look at new conflicts as complex socio-economic phenomena based and supported by war economy and the 'manufacturing of identities' (Kaldor 2007). The first group of scholars gives emphasis to the economic interests and mechanisms at stake and is likely to suggest an institutional cosmopolitanism; while the second, emphasizing the political significance of constructed identities, stresses the important role played by informal non-governmental entities in such conflicts.

(1) According to the first perspective, which I call economic perspective, it would be possible to understand the dynamics of such wars taking into account the complex relationship existing between 'greed' and 'grievances' (Collier and Hoeffler 2004, Collier et al. 2006). Greed is used in such context as a desire for

private gain. For Collier, the war represents a mean to achieve economic benefits. The combination of large exports of primary commodities, since these sources are in general 'lootable' assets (diamonds, drugs, oil), and the high proportion of young men, since under certain conditions fighting is the only form of employment, combined with a situation of economic decline, drastically increase the risk of conflict (Collier 2004). Once the war starts the cycle of violence and deprivations produces grievances and economic destruction, which make such conflict difficult to stop.

Other authors draw attention to the role played by warlords who, often helped and supported by international actors, fuel the conflict for economic reasons. According to them, 'new wars' are the product of the distortion of the late capitalism applied to weak or failing states: the interests of warlords often overlap with that of transnational companies and this allows warlords and war criminals to secure domestic legitimization and make use of external support. In this context, deregulation rules of market economy are associated with forms of 'illiberal' religious or ethnic fundamentalism that easily translates into collapse of the rule of law, authoritarianism and widespread human rights abuse (Duffield 1998). In other terms, what in the West is supposed to be senseless violence is actually a rational response to economic, social and political circumstances (Duffield 1998; Keen 1998; Duffield 2002). The economic perspective emphasizes the global 'dimension' of such new wars and argues for a genuine cosmopolitan politics that endorses international law and the search for 'participatory common values' (Duffield 2001). Therefore, the international community should foster inclusive political arrangements supplemented by robust economic and military external assistance (Collier et al. 2006).

(2) The second group of scholars focuses attention on the links between political purposes and constructed identities. According to them, the new wave of nationalism and religious ideologies represents the key feature of new wars, and it has to be understood as the product of new constructed rivalries (Kaldor 1999, 2004, 2005; Kaldor et al. 2007). If the sectarian identities are constructed, rather than given, the idea of an 'unavoidable struggle between the West and rest' based on the idea of ancient hatreds loses any significance. Therefore, the answer to 'new wars' resides in strengthening those actors in civil society who promote a non-sectarian identity, i.e. cosmopolitan groups, human rights groups or women's groups (Kaldor 2003a). During the last two decades, a global civil society, bearer of democratic values, has emerged as a transnational response to violence. According to these scholars, such civil society actors play a pivotal role in transforming the war economies and constructing non-sectarian identities.

2.1.3 'New and old wars: a valid distinction?'[6]

Following the two approaches described before, ethno-religious conflicts are supposed to be mainly a new phenomenon that, emerging during the last two decades from the ruins of the Soviet system, has been further emphasized by the dynamics of globalization. If we look at Table 1, it is clear that prima facie the two approaches share at least two elements: the external causes and the violence's impact. In addition to this, it is possible to note that there is a further analogy, or at least similarity, with regard to the fourth point. The fact that the targeted victims are 'other cultural groups' or 'civilizations', in fact, does not contradict the fact that they can be civilians and non-combatants.

What is evident here is that, despite the differences in the internal causes and in the answers/outcomes, these alleged contrasting approaches are not so different, as their scholars would claim. Actually, on the one hand they consider ethno-religious conflicts as phenomena deeply rooted in globalization processes, that is why they call such conflicts 'new wars/new struggles/new challenges'; while, on the other hand, they seek to offer different answers, post-statism/cultural relativism vs cosmopolitanism/universalist view, coherent with the post–Cold War international system. Conversely, the major difference concerns the link between violence and identity. Post-statism introduces an essentialist account of cultural identity. On the contrary, the second approach explains sectarian violence as rationally constructed by groups/elites/warlords. Identity and its attributions, in this context, are seen as the product of a social construction.

Therefore, without considering the *vexata questio* about the link between violence and identity, it is possible to recognize a first crucial feature emerging from the recent scholarly work about ethno-religious conflicts. Ethnic or religious differences, typical of such new wars, are being exacerbated and fuelled by globalization processes. Accordingly, ethnic and religious identities, whether primordial or constructed, would intervene in conflicts because of a dramatic rise in intensity and the extent of political, cultural and economic interconnection that has occurred since the end of the Cold War.

The problem here is to understand if this first assumption, which associates ethno-religious conflicts to globalization, can be useful for our analysis. In other terms, if it is possible to assert that the recent wars in Bosnia, Kosovo, Chechnya, Rwanda and Darfur hide an 'essential similarity' in their close link with economic, political or cultural dynamics put into action by globalization. This issue is relevant because it leads scholars to divert the attention from the alleged link between violence and identity, which seems to be weird and devious, focusing on dynamics that can be managed through political actions. But, is this idea acceptable? Is there a concrete causal link between globalization and ethno-religious conflicts? Can we distinguish between old and new civil wars, considering the religious/ethnic character as the product of the present age?

Undoubtedly, globalization has had a huge impact on conflicts and violence. The communications revolution has decreased distances among countries, regions and continents, encouraging the emergence of a new sensitivity towards the 'others'. The new role of media was clear since the first months of the siege of Sarajevo, in May 1992, when a plethora of foreign journalists went to Bosnia to show to the rest of the world the worst European massacre after the Second World War. In this context, a new kind of journalism of war has emerged, which aimed at placing the stories of real people at the centre of history and at establishing sympathetic links between victims of the wars and ordinary people (Bennett 2007). Additionally, the new imbalances in global and domestic economies have contributed to the collapse of newly emerged states in Africa, Asia and Eastern Europe, increasing the number of failed or failing states that are more likely to degenerate into violent conflicts. Lastly, the phenomenon of mass migration has created new political and cultural fault lines and, in some circumstances, new opportunities for fundamentalists, rebels and terrorists. All these factors have had, in various ways, relevant effects on ethno-religious wars, but, again, this is not enough to maintain the alleged causal link between ethno-religious violence and globalization.

In fact, several empirical studies have recently demonstrated the inconsistencies of this view. Empirical evidences show that the rates of civil wars involving groups of different ethnic or religious identities were identical before and after the Cold War; furthermore, they pointed out that most of these wars began in the 1960s (Russett et al. 2000). Similarly, Melander, Oberg and Hall (2009) have shown that the peak in the number of ethno-religious conflicts from 1989 to 1992 reflects the changed situation in Europe after the collapse of the Soviet Union, therefore it can be associated with the emergence of new national entities rather than globalization processes. In addition, they argue that the general number of ethno-religious conflicts has decreased from 1991 to 2001 (ibid.).

From a theoretical point of view, Kalyvas criticizes the distinction 'new/old wars' that in his view would be based on 'un-critical adoption of categories and labels grounded in mischaracterizations' (Kalyvas 2001: 99). Accordingly, the distinction between 'post-Cold War conflicts and their predecessor' (ibid.) would be related more to the lack of conceptual political categories applicable to the post–Cold War era than to any structural shift in the nature of war. Some scholars, then, suggest that a longer historical perspective would reveal that most of the recent conflicts are comparable in the purposes and causes to those that occurred in the last two centuries linked to the demise of empires and their replacement by a system of sovereign nation-states.

Violent internal conflict, rather than linked to globalization processes, can be understood as a product of processes associated with the creation of nation-states.

> [...] Indeed, many of [these] conflicts [...] have occurred in places where the nation-state form has only recently been introduced, where the nation-building project is incomplete or in transition, where the attempts to build nation states have failed [...], or where nationalist movements pursue secession and seek their own nation-state" (Min and Wimmer 2007: 73).

Similarly, Ayoob, arguing the close link between contemporary conflicts and the dynamics of state making (state breaking and failure), stresses the 'essential similarity' of the episodes of violence experienced by Third World countries today and the European history of the last centuries. According to him, such similarity would demonstrate the intrinsic violence of this process that in 'Western Europe cost tremendously in death, suffering, loss of rights, and unwilling surrender of lands, goods or labor' (Ayoob 1996: 130).

In the light of such criticisms, it seems that the supporters of the 'new wars' paradigm tend to confuse the general context, globalization, with the actual cause of the phenomenon. As shown in the present section, even if it is hard to deny any impact of globalization on recent ethno-religious conflicts, nevertheless it may be misleading to believe that globalization, *per se*, ignites identitarian violence. In order to clarify this point, one can consider the cases of the Lebanese civil war of 1975 and the Bosnian war of 1992.

Undoubtedly, an approach focused on globalization would take the case of the war in Bosnia as example of 'new war' and therefore it would deny any kind of comparison with the case of the Lebanese civil war. For Kaldor, for instance, the war in Bosnia is 'the archetypal example, the paradigm of a new kind of warfare' (Kaldor 1999: 33). According to her, that war mobilized a huge international effort and it was a terrain to test new ideologies and new spectacular forms of violence. Nevertheless, Lebanon and Bosnia share the same historical tradition of religious pluralism and tolerance in the context of the Ottoman Empire, and, in both cases, this tradition seemed to vanish when they became nation-states. However, while the Ottoman Empire was replaced in Bosnia by another form of 'multinational' state, the former Yugoslavia, in the case of Lebanon this shift happened soon after the end the Second World War. Following the arguments of Ayoob (1996) and Wimmer et al. (2006), the explosion of violence and internal wars in both countries would be easily understandable in the light of the effects of nation-state making; as soon as the process of nation-state making in these two countries began, in fact, it was followed by violent riots.

Two further elements would confirm the thesis of similarity rather than incompatibility between the two cases: the religious character of the fighters and the external interventions. (1) In both conflicts the combatants were defined in religious terms, Maronite-Christians against the coalition of Shi'a Sunni and Druze Islamic militias in Lebanon, while in Bosnia the main actors were the Serb-Orthodox army of the Srpska Republic (hereafter VRS), the Croat-Christian militia (hereafter HVO), and the Bosniak-Muslim Army of the Republic of Bosnia and Herzegovina (henceforth ABiH). (2) In both cases, external interventionism played a crucial role in characterizing the form of violence. In the Lebanese conflict, Syria and Israel had an active role during all phases of the war originating an actual military balance aimed mainly at precluding a competitor gaining an advantage; while in Bosnia the same role was played by Croatia and Serbia. The Serb leader Milosevic and the Croat Tudjman were deeply involved in the planning of the systematic ethnic cleansing through the region and in supporting and controlling the military and paramilitary Croat and Serb groups active in Bosnia during the conflict. Furthermore, in both cases the interests of other state-actors were framed in the context of the existing religious rivalries.

This example shows again that globalization processes cannot be considered as the cause of religious or ethnic violence and that a distinction between 'new' and 'old' wars is, at least, questionable. Indeed, it shows that such arguments effectively diverted the attention from the relevant issue at stake, which concerns the identity–violence nexus. Again, the cases of Lebanon and Bosnia show that identity politics still plays a central role in these countries. In this perspective, the efforts in deconstructing nationalism and valorizing betrayed tradition 'led some authors to oversimplify the history of interethnic relations in Bosnia' (Bougarel and Duijzings 2007: 11). Furthermore, what is even more dangerous, it led them to disregard the role of memory, myths and symbols of the recent war, which have a huge impact on Bosnian society fuelling a mosaic of clashing identities. In the next section, I discuss the meaning of identity in the light of recent scholarly work, and I seek to deepen the link between identity and violence.

2. 2
CONFLICTS OVER IDENTITY CLAIMS:
EXPLORING THE MEANING OF IDENTITY IN CONFLICT

Theories of conflict resolution have shown a growing attention towards the link between identity and violence as an underlying cause of violent conflict. The PSC theory was developed by Azar and Burton from the 1970s to the 1990s (Gurr 1994, 2001; Ramsbotham 2005). According to these scholars, the emergence of identity-conflicts imposes upon us to reconsider the levels of the analysis — generally based on the state level — focusing on the communal level.[7] Multicommunal societies, mostly postcolonial states, are characterized by the 'prolonged and often violent struggles among different communal groups for some "basic needs", such as security, recognition, and acceptance, fair access to political institution and economic participation' (Azar 1990: 93). This approach looks at identity groups — i.e. ethnic, religious, or racial groups — as the most useful unit of analysis; 'ethnic heterogeneity' is therefore understood as a 'structural precondition' for ethno-religious conflicts (Gurr 2001, 2007).

In the 1990s, Johan Galtung introduced 'cultural violence' in his influential model of conflict, violence and peace (Galtung 1990, 1996). Cultural violence was defined by Galtung as any aspect of a culture that can be used to legitimize violence.[8] In contrast to a sort of biological determinism, his understanding of cultural violence was referred to 'those aspects' (Galtung 1990: 294) – i.e. stars, crosses and crescents or flags, anthems and military parades – aimed at legitimizing violence. His study of cultural violence displays how the act of direct violence (people are killed) and the fact of structural violence (people die through poverty and exclusion) are linked to each other and legitimized by the cultural dimension. The interdependence of the three forms of violence is represented as a triangle, with structural violence (A), direct violence (B) and cultural violence (C) at its vertices.

Direct violence should be therefore interpreted as the event, structural violence as the process and cultural violence as the invariant, 'remaining essentially the same for long periods' (Galtung 1990: 294). Due to such a scheme, one can explain situations of protracted structural violence supported by ideological and cultural arguments. With regard to the case of the African slaves, Galtung shows how a deep understanding of the role of direct (the Africans were captured, forced across the Atlantic to work as slaves, most of them were killed and tortured in the process), structural (whites as the 'master top-dogs' and blacks as the 'slave underdogs') and cultural (racist ideas) violence could explain the phenomena of 'discrimination' and 'prejudice' that affected contemporary American society.

Azar and Galtung's intuitions have inspired important developments in literature about the role of identity in conflict. Rothman distinguishes a new category of conflicts, which he calls *identity-conflicts*. These conflicts diverge from interest-based disputes. While interest-based conflicts tend to be more concrete, the issues more clearly defined, and the potential for mutual benefit more obvious, identity-based conflicts would be based on people's psychology, culture, basic values, shared history and beliefs. According to him, identity-conflicts threaten people's basic needs and very survival (Rothman 1997; Rothman and Olson 2001). For Sambanis (2001) identity-conflicts are predominantly rooted in political and social grievances rather than the lack of economic opportunities. Other studies have shown the special link between religious cleavages and violence. This would partially explain why intergroup conflict so frequently occurs along religious fault lines (Seul 1999).

A prudential view is then offered by Kalyvas, who describes identity-conflicts in terms of interactions between political and private identities and actions. In this perspective, master cleavages, of religious or ethnic matrix, emerging from the conflict would represent a sort of 'symbolic formation' that simplifies and encompasses several local conflicts. These local conflicts seem to be linked to peripheral or 'private issues' rather than collective public claims (Kalyvas 2003, 2007).

In general, however, the approaches to new wars illustrated in the last section tend to offer two different understandings of identity. What I called a culturalist account focuses on an essentialist view of 'ancient hatreds', while the second approach insists on an idea of socially constructed identities. Contemporary literature about identity-conflicts therefore shows a

> long-standing difference of approach between those who see ethnic groups as firmly bounded, durable communities inclined toward ethnocentrism, hostility to outsiders, and passionate conflict, and those who see them as social constructs, with a solidarity based on material rewards and conflict behaviour based on calculation (Horowitz 1998, 2001).[9]

In the next section, I analyze the phenomenon of ethno-religious conflicts in the light of a deeper understanding of the meaning of identity. After a preliminary examination of the two contemporary approaches to identity, I offer a third perspective about identity seen as the result of multiple identities. In particular, it is important to see how identity, understood as the sum of plural affiliations, interacts with economic and political features in the context of internal conflicts. The second issue, instead, concerns the link between identity and violence.

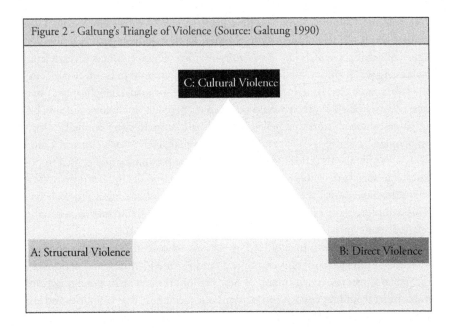

Figure 2 - Galtung's Triangle of Violence (Source: Galtung 1990)

2.2.1 A deeper understanding of identity: two forms of reductionism and plural affiliations

The contemporary debate over identity in political theory has wandered from the actual research about the nature of cultural attributions, whether given or constructed, seeking to place emphasis on the link between such attributions and individuals. It is possible to distinguish two different positions that emerge in this debate: the first, deeply rooted in Kantian philosophy, is focused on the role of personal autonomy at the root of individualism; while the second, linked to the Hegelian understanding of history, privileges an organicist account of society. In the light of this distinction, the key issue has been represented by the identification of agents in the political realm, whether collectives or individuals. In this perspective, liberal approaches have tended to consider the individual as the underlying subject of politics (Rawls 1971), while communitarian perspectives have emphasized the intrinsic value of the community, since a historically rooted culture represented, in their view, the necessary precondition for individualism (Taylor 1994; Sandel 1982).

Despite these differences, both approaches have been shown to pay growing attention to the issue of the integration of citizens in contemporary plural societies. In the context of liberal theory, the emergence of new awareness about cultural differences can be traced back to Rawls's notions of reasonable pluralism and overlapping consensus (Rawls 2005). These ideas originated a huge literature focused on the possibilities of accommodating cultural and ethnic claims into the liberal political theory; in some sense, the debate between communitarians and liberals evolved into a discussion about the impact and the inclusion of non-Western tradition and minorities into Western liberal societies (Kymlicka 1996). In one sense, contemporary approaches to multiculturalism tend to neglect the nature of the identitarian affiliations, constructed or given, giving priority to the way in which it is possible to include and accommodate such claims in the broader frame of liberalism (May et al. 2004).

As shown in the last section, identity has played, instead, a pivotal role in discussing and interpreting identity-conflicts in contemporary conflict theories. Accordingly, two different versions of identity have emerged: on the one hand, a primordial approach that sees ethnic or religious groups as deeply rooted, long-lasting communities prone to high levels of hostility to outsiders and fanatical conflict; the second approach, instead, sees them as social constructs, with an idea of solidarity based on material advantages and rational understanding of behaviour in conflict situations. Thus, what does identity mean? When and why does identity, whether constructed or primordial, interact with violence? Furthermore, what is the role of individuals in such a framework?

In order to offer adequate answers to these questions, it is necessary to investigate the content of identity. It is possible to distinguish two different forms of reductionism: cultural reductionism and individualist reductionism.[10] For cultural reductionism individuals are not separate units, rather they are deeply embedded in larger groups (i.e. extended family, village, ethnic or religious community). In this view, it is impossible to describe individuals' actions and motivations without considering the significance of their shared identity. Conversely, individualist reductionism represents its opposite version. Such a reductionism shows a complete lack of interest about identity and its cultural implications. This approach looks at the individuals as main subjects of any political action. Individuals' actions are based on rational calculations and interests. In such a framework, identity becomes an irrelevant variable.

As shown in the last section, when applied to identity-conflicts, cultural reductionism emphasizes the ancient cultural hatreds, while individualist reductionism treats identitarian features as the result of a social construction. Common sense might lead us to lean towards the second approach, since it assumes an individualistic account. Nevertheless, the idea that individuals are independent islands is highly problematic: it seems difficult to isolate individuals' actions and motivations from the collective and ideological dimension of violence (Kalyvas

2003). At the same time, the emphasis on cultural differences among groups would lead to the extreme relativistic assumption that cultural heterogeneity itself is at the roots of ethnic or religious conflicts (Huntington 1996).

It seems therefore necessary to offer a third view about identity, and its implications in conflict. Following Sen's thesis on the identity and violence nexus (Sen 2006), it may be more plausible to argue that individuals hold multiple identities.[11] Ethnic and religious features simply are attributions of individual identity. Each individual is the result of a complex set of multiple identities, e.g. gender, political ideology, religious beliefs, nationality, race, caste, and ethnic affiliations. Persons cannot be isolated from the emotional side of their shared identities: it would be otherwise impossible to explain the human experiences of people like Nelson Mandela, Mother Teresa, or Gandhi (ibid.).

At the same time, focusing attention on one identity is not enough in order to explain the complexity of such human experiences. Let's consider the example of Mother Teresa: her life can hardly be explained in rational terms, nonetheless it is abundantly clear that her religious affiliation, Christian Catholicism, is not enough to explain her experience as missionary of charity. She defined herself as a woman ('I am a woman'), as an Albanian ('by blood, I am Albanian') but also as an Indian by adoption ('by citizenship, an Indian'), as a Catholic by faith ('By faith, I am a Catholic nun') and — what is more important — as a part of the human community ('As to my calling, I belong to the world'). The combination of all these attributions makes Mother Teresa's experience so unique and unrepeatable.

While a communitarian account might lead to underestimate the role of individuals giving priority to a set of cultural and historical preconditions already present in the society, an approach based on the idea of multiple identities does not deny the freedom to choose about the relative weight to confer to the different affiliations (Sen 2006a). This notion relies on a complex conception of the self: a self that freely chooses and revises its preferences and life plans, on the one hand, and a self that recognizes itself and is shaped in relation to collective identities. However, although the issue of freedom of choice is crucial in the framework of plural identities, it is important to clarify how it is possible to make a decision in this sense and, moreover, to what extent. As Sen argues, the issue at stake is not related to the freedom of individuals to select any identity; to be more precise, the *freedom of choice* concerns the possibility to give priority to one or more over the entire set of identities that each individual simultaneously possesses (Sen 2006a). Mother Teresa gave priority to her vocation to help human beings, and her feeling of belonging to the world over, for example, her Albanian nationality.

Therefore, what is the link between identitarian affiliations and violence? The idea of multiple identities, as such, does not say anything about the link between identity and violence. Therefore, it becomes important to understand how and why in several internal conflicts some cultural features — as for instance ethnicity, race or religion — are likely to overcome other affiliations interacting with violence. Neither ethnicity, nor race, nor religion can be considered as violent factors, per se. The fact that an individual is black or white, Christian or Muslim, Croat or Serb, does not explain anything about herself or himself; the combination of all her/his affiliations makes recognizable an individual and her/his human experience. Nevertheless, the evidence of contemporary conflicts seems to say that these factors are inherently violent. Actually, it would be very dangerous to assert such an idea; the history of humanity, starting from the Christian Crusades, to Hitler's eugenic plan for a master race, is in fact studded with examples of violence hidden behind cultures, religions and racial or ethnic features.

In the next sections, I will explain this phenomenon in the light of three distinct arguments: the cultural rooted idea of nation, the 'spread condition' of capability-deprivation within society, the role of cultural-war-entrepreneurs in fuelling sectarian violence.

2.2.2 Internal conflicts: the meaning of nation and plural identities

In contrast with both reductionisms, I have emphasized the necessity to understand identity as a plural and flexible concept. The issue is therefore to identify why and how some identities, namely religious, ethno-linguistic or nationalistic affiliations, tend to interact with violence in internal conflicts. In this perspective, a clarification first has to be made with respect to the idea of *nation*. The analysis of the idea of *nation* shows a longstanding link between this concept and some particular affiliations, namely ethnicity/race, language and religion.

The argument can be developed in the following way. One person can be Indian, English speaking, and Muslim, without any contradiction. In everyday life, it is possible to discover a boundless variety of combinations of different affiliations. Nevertheless, within national boundaries such affiliations are likely to become more relevant. Within Italian boundaries, a French-speaking citizen may be considered as part of a minority group: this is because in the alleged definition of Italian nationality the language represents a factor of strong cultural identification. In this respect, Hobsbawm emphasized,

> for Germans and Italians, their national language was not merely an administrative convenience, or a means of unifying state-wide communication [...] it was even more the vehicle of a distinguished literature and

of universal intellectual expression. It was the only thing that made them Germans or Italians [...]. (Hutchinson and Smith 1994: 177).

Of course, this was true not only for Italians and for Germans. In contrast with the vastly invoked distinction between *cultural nations* and *civic nations* (Ignatieff 2003; Hutchinson and Smith 1994), my thesis is that the early contemporary notion of *nation* always involves specific cultural features, which function as a kind of cultural 'glue' between people and territory. This explains why, in several contemporary internal conflicts, some cultural affiliations, namely ethnicity, language, religion, are likely to become so relevant.

The term *nation* is a derivative of the much older Latin word *natio-nis*, which in turn was formed from the verb *nascor-nasci*. Therefore, it was originally related to an idea of 'birth'. In the Latin usage *natio* referred to the barbarian or distant people, while the Romans used to define themselves in terms of *populus* (Hutchinson 1996). The word came back into use at the end of the eighteenth century after the American and French revolutions. Although there was no agreement among scholars about its actual content, the first supporters of the idea of *nation*, such as Rousseau, Herder, Fichte and Mazzini, recovered from the ancient tradition the idea of birth, the link with territory, emphasizing three main attributions: autonomy, unity and identity (Hutchinson and Smith 1994).

In his influential work, Renan offered an idea of nation as a form of morality, 'a great aggregation of men, with a healthy spirit and warmth of heart, creates a moral conscience which is called a *nation*'.[12] Weber defined the nation as a 'prestige community'; according to him '[...] one might well define the concept of *nation* in the following way: a *nation* is a community of sentiment which would adequately manifest itself in a state of its own; hence, a *nation* is community which normally tends to produce a state of its own'.[13] Furthermore, according to Stalin a nation was a 'historically constituted, stable community of people, formed on the basis of a common language, territory, economic life [...]'.[14] Gradually, the idea of nation started to indicate the association of cultural and historical developments of societies with the territory where those societies used to live.

Conversely, contemporary scholars tend to make a distinction between civic nations, based on the idea of political community, i.e. France or the United States, and cultural nations, based on a certain degree of cultural unity, i.e. Iran or Israel. This distinction is based on the assumption that some contemporary examples of nationalism are concerned with political principles rather than cultural features (Ignatieff 1993, 1997). Indeed, the role of cultural features, as for instance language, in the alleged civic nations cannot be dismissed as mere administrative convenience or method of unifying communication across society. If we look at the French case, which is often employed as a typical example of a civic nation, it is worth noticing that at least one cultural feature, the common language, was brutally imposed on Basques, Bretons and other linguistic minorities with the clear goal of creating a 'common French identity' (Kymlicka 2001: 244). Thus, French nationalism, as many other cases of alleged civic nationalism, has been rooted not only in political principles, such as equality and freedom, but also in a shared French culture, based on the linguistic homogeneity. As Kymlicka has argued 'promoting a common sense of history is a way of ensuring [...] people identity, not just with abstract principles, but with this political community, with its particular boundaries, institutions, procedures, and so on' (ibid.: 245).

Nationalism is thus always concerned with culture; however, such cultural features are likely to become more relevant in the absence of a strong democratic system. Actually, in a liberal-democratic society, the special link between some specific cultural features and the idea of nation is mitigated by the democratic principles themselves. Conversely, in deeply divided states — mostly post-conflict societies, post-colonial countries or former multinational states — where the balance between democratic principles and cultural features is still weak or totally absent, cultural attributions strongly influence the idea of nation, and the conflicts over its boundaries.

Thus, while in Western societies cultural boundaries have been expressed mostly in ethno-linguistic terms, in most of the rest of the world, especially in undemocratic countries or in contexts where a civic-democratic tradition is still weak, the religious and ethno-racial aspects tend to overlap with the boundaries of the nation. This difference introduces two distinct arguments: the first argument is concerned with the liberal interpretation of nation-state as developed in contemporary Western societies, while the second is more concerned with the post-colonial critique. First, in modern liberal democratic societies, a special link between some specific religious beliefs or ethnic affiliations and the idea of nation would be in contrast to the democratic principles of equality and neutrality of the state towards its citizens. Second, in most of the post-colonial countries as well as in former multinational states, ethnic language alone does not express that special link with the territory. In some sense, the Western category of nation has been thus associated to other cultural aspects more relevant in these contexts. It is difficult to generalize this argument, but it seems to be possible to apply this idea to several cases in Africa, in the Balkans and Middle East, as well as in Asia.

To consider the case of former colonial empires in Asia and Africa, the official language was mostly imposed by the colonizers, and, therefore, it represented a sort of external element. Only later, the process of decolonization would have revealed the presence of several unofficial dialects or languages. As a consequence, the adoption of the language of the former colonial empires as the official one became a convenient solution for administrative and communicative reasons.[15] This may explain why in most of these countries religious or ethnic features, rather than language, have become cultural attributions of the idea of nation or nationality.

As for the Balkans, it is worth noticing the strong impact that the administrative arrangements of the Ottoman Empire had on the idea of ethno-language in this region. The Ottoman Millet system was a complex set of administrative arrangements that the Ottomans put into action in order to deal with non-Muslim communities, which lived under the protection of the sovereign Muslim state. In particular, this system was thought up with respect to specific religious minorities, the so-called *Dhimmis*, made up of those non-Muslims who believed in the Bible, namely Orthodox Christians, Catholic Christians and Jews. The constitution of different Millets, which were based on the religious difference, was aimed at guaranteeing a certain degree of autonomy to those religious communities in terms of rights and liberties. In turn, they had to pay a special tax for this religious autonomy. In this system, religious and linguistic elements were generally considered as deeply linked each other (Aral 2004).

Undoubtedly, in internal conflicts the issue of territory plays a crucial role, and a deeper understanding of the idea of nation in terms of the link between some cultural and historical aspects and territory can offer a way to understand why some affiliations, namely religion, ethnicity or language, tend to emerge as relevant features in internal conflicts. In some sense, the connection between such identities and specific territories can clarify the meaning of what I call the 'mobilizing power of identity-based arguments'.

However, this understanding of nation, territory and cultural elements, alone, cannot explain the outbreak of violence. In the next sections, I consider the identity–violence nexus as a consequence of two distinct factors. On the one hand, the lack of freedom and democratic rules aimed at protecting individuals and their socio-economic, political and cultural rights produces a condition of social grievances within population. On the other, I look at the role of private associations and individuals, which I call 'cultural-war-entrepreneurs'; these actors are likely to manipulate the masses into fuelling identity-based violence.

2.3
IDENTITY IN CONFLICT:
LACK OF FREEDOMS AND THE LIMITS OF RATIONALITY

In this last section, I develop an argument in favour of an understanding of identity-conflicts, where identity is seen as the sum of plural affiliations (Sen 2006a). I first show the limits of the two forms of reductionism testing them to the case of Bosnian conflict. I therefore distinguish two arguments. (1) The first argument considers the social grievances linked to lack of recognition and free expression of identitarian affiliations within society, which, associated to the lack of political freedoms and economic opportunities, creates the conditions for an identity-conflict. (2) The second argument focuses on the demagogic use of identity-based arguments made by 'cultural-war-entrepreneurs' as the actual source of violence; but, in contrast to constructivists' view I consider violence as the result of the failure of rationality.

These two arguments are profoundly linked to each other; very often, the so-called 'identitarian associations' reinvent the mythology of the losers for hiding their interests and purposes. This dynamic creates a condition for what Foucault (2003) called 'permanent war' in which the racist/religious arguments become part of power's dialectic that is perpetuated in 'peace time' by local politicians and the international community. Often, the difficulty in understanding and facing such conflicts depends on the fact that both practitioners and scholars underestimate the effects of such a sort of 'bio-power' on deeply divided societies. As pointed out by Azar (1990), in fact, it is necessary to pay attention to the covert, latent, and often non-violent side of such conflicts in order to understand them.

2.3.1 The two reductionisms applied to conflicts

In the previous section, I have discussed two different ways to look at the issue of identity in conflict that emerged from the contemporary scholarly debate. The culturalist approach suggests a primordialist understanding of identity, I have called this cultural reductionism. Conversely, rational choice scholars are inclined to see identity issues in conflict as rationally constructed; this presupposes a second form of reductionism that I have called individualist reductionism. The present section is aimed at testing the two reductionisms discussed before in the framework of a concrete case of conflict — the case of the Bosnian civil war of 1992–95.

(1) Following the first kind of reductionism, the war in Bosnia might be considered as a clear example of communal conflict (Gurr 2007). This conflict was characterized by the violent confrontation among the three religious communities, namely Orthodox Christian Serbs, Roman Catholic Croats and Muslim Bosniaks supported by their respective co-religionists in other parts of the world. Such a case would therefore demonstrate that ethnic heterogeneity, rooted in this case in religious antagonism, is likely to become a 'structural precondition for ethnic warfare' (Gurr et al. 2005: 2).

Nevertheless, evidences demonstrate that the explanatory value of religious heterogeneity in Bosnian war is limited. As pointed out by Powers (1996) the religious dimension of this conflict is often exaggerated. Despite the religious differences within the three groups, it is worth noticing that the actual involvement of religious actors (priests, bishops or imams) was quite rare and, in general, religious leaders themselves did not conceive of the conflict in religious terms.[16] Actually, several studies have shown that a 'Bosnian pluralistic society' had existed for centuries, and, despite the differences in their 'religious backgrounds', a Bosnian shared culture, based on a linguistic, ethnic and historical unity had been a reality for ages (Bougarel 1996, Donia and Fine 1994).[17] Furthermore, 50 years of a secular Yugoslav state had a huge impact in fostering the secularization of society; with reference to this, Fine has argued that only 'few modern-day Bosnians (and certainly almost none of those leading any of the sides in the current war) are deeply religious' (Donia and Fine 1994: 9).

Actually, an approach too focused on the relevance of ethnic or religious heterogeneity might lead to underrate the actual *use* and *misuse* of religious differences as a part of the ethno- mobilization strategy that the three political leaders, i.e. Milosević, Tudjman and Izetbegović, put into action in the 1990s. During the war, religious affiliation represented a way to differentiate people; religion became a means of mass mobilization largely employed by political leaders (Powers 1996). Indeed, in several cases religious lines were crossed by fighters who found it convenient to dismiss community boundaries for private interests. Quite notorious is the case of the Bosniak leader Fikret Abdic (Kalyvas and Sambanis 2005). Obtaining the control over the area of Bihac (North-Western Bosnia), he fought with Serbs against the army of the Central Bosnian Government. In addition, it is widely recognized that most of the fighters were ordinary criminals rather than religious fundamentalists. The Serb warlord Arkan, as well as the Bosniak leaders Ramiz Delic ('Celo'), Musan Topalovic ('Caco'), Jusuf Prazina ('Juka') had criminal backgrounds; as Kalyvas and Sambanis have argued, 'the first to embrace the violence of the war were those who had embraced it in peace' (ibid.: 215, see also Kaldor 1999).

(2) With reference to the second form of reductionism, it is possible to distinguish the economic approach to 'greed vs grievances' from what I call the political account to 'new nationalisms'. In both approaches individuals' actions and interests play a fundamental role. However, while if for the economic approach, some economic factors are crucial causes of civil wars, the approach to 'new nationalisms' is more focused on the role of political leaders in constructing sectarian identities and ideologies (Kaldor 1999, 2003a, 2003b).[18] However, in both versions also this second form of reductionism can hardly explain some relevant features of Bosnian conflict.

Table 2 - Incomes and inequalities former Yugoslavia 1988-1990						
COUNTRY	1988 INCOME PER CAPITA (PA)	1990 INCOME PER CAPITA (US $)	POPULATION 1990	REL. INCOME 1988	REL. INCOME 1990	GINI (1988 INCOME)
BiH	2,124,319	2,365	3,516	76,2	67,8	24,4
Montenegro	2,062,042	2,484	644	73,9	71,1	25,6
Croatia	3,234,631	4,468	4,685	116,0	127,8	22,1
Macedonia	1,790,902	2,282	2,131	64,2	65,3	30,9
Slovenia	5,529,722	7,610	1,953	198,3	217,7	19,3
Serbia	2,523,329	3,379	5,849	90,5	96,7	25,0
Kosovo	1,062,039	854	1,983	38,1	24,4	27,7
Vojvodina	3,166,398	4,320	2,048	113,6	123,6	26,5
Yugoslavia	2,788,443	3,496	23,809	100,0	100,0	24,5
Source: Kalyvas & Sambanis 2005						

(i) According to the economic approach, poverty is a key variable in predicting identity-conflicts. By the end of the 1980s, Yugoslavian regions had to face the effects of a severe economic crisis that fuelled a process of hyperinflation and increased the levels of unemployment.[19] Nevertheless, as Table 2 shows, the economic situation in Bosnia from 1988 to 1990, compared with that of other regions (Kosovo or Macedonia), does not seem to be significant in terms of poverty. Therefore, even though high levels of poverty might be conducive to political violence, this cannot be assumed as a rule for all conflicts.

Indeed, the high level of inequalities among and within the regions, rather than poverty as such, was conducive to the conflicts of the 1990s in former Yugoslavia. As Kalyvas and Sambanis show (2005: 206-7), 'the fact that rich yet small (in terms of population) regions provided the bulk of fiscal transfer to poorer, larger regions generated an incentive for secession in the richer regions' Furthermore, in Bosnia, more than in other regions given its mountainous morphology, the differences in both incomes and levels of education between rural and urban areas was a key structural precondition for the conflict. This would explain why some authors have referred to the war in terms of 'revenge of the countryside' (Bougarel 1999: 157). Finally, it is worth noticing that Bosnia had no natural resources of note (Kalyvas and Sambanis 2005). In addition, it is widely recognized that the main wartime economic activities were based on robberies, criminal actions and trade of prisoners with enemies, rather than on the exports of 'lootable' resources (Andreas 2004).

(ii) On the other hand, the political approach to 'new nationalisms' raises a further problem, since it does not take into account what I call the 'mobilizing power of identity-based arguments'. Although the role of authoritarian leaders and common criminals was significant during the war, the actual involvement of citizens and non-combatants, more so in rural regions, was massive. This was due to the mobilizing power that religious arguments had in this war. During a recent field trip in Sarajevo, I interviewed several groups of survivors and relatives of the victims.[20] It might be useful to report here some pieces of one of these interviews, which is very instructive in order to understand the meaning of what I call mobilizing power of identity-based arguments.

> After a few weeks of bombardment, the Serbs occupied the municipality of Vogošća; I was captured and brought to a concentration camp. [...] Every night, the jailers of the camp forced me and other women to go to the city centre [...] We were asked to steal from our houses. [...] One night, I met the husband of my best friend. We spent all our life together... we were really good friends and I thought it was a miracle to meet him! I was sure he could have helped me and my kids to run away. [...] But, before I could say any word he told me *"Woman go away, otherwise I will kill you!*[21] [Emphasis added]

This experience shows the difference between actions and interests of political leaders and the behaviour of ordinary people. Actually, mobilization practices of authoritarian leaders and criminals can only partly explain the phenomenon; evidences demonstrate that identitarian arguments *per se* were more likely to create boundaries among the three groups during that war.

Finally, a further theoretical argument against this second form of reductionism is concerned with the idea of 'rationality'. We could define at least three conceptions of rationality. At the weakest level, all actions are rational so long as the individual is using them to achieve predetermined ends. At a second level, we could define a standard economic approach where rationality requires that individuals choose the best action according to the utility function. Lastly, a more sophisticated definition of rationality requires that individuals respond to incentive and behave according to rational expectations. An important condition in all these versions is that choices and behaviours can be ineffective, and thus irrational, because of erroneous information, lack of information, or unpredictable complexity in the external world (Berrebi 2009). Therefore the 'rational-choice approach' to conflict generally is based on two assumptions: (i) the existence of self-interested individuals, (ii) who act according to a strict costs-benefits calculus with respect to goals and means. However, this idea of 'rationality' is highly problematic in actual societies where the rational behaviour based on the costs-benefits calculus is mitigated by behaviours and actions which respond to what Weber had defined as 'a conscious ethical, aesthetic, religious or other belief, independently of its prospects of success' (Varshney 2003b: 86).

The idea of isolating a rational, value-free and self-interested individual from any tie, shared value or belief, is not only unrealistic but also not convincing. As rightly pointed out by Varshney, in philosophy rationality is almost referred to 'reasoned assessment as the basis of action' (ibid.: 86), but this 'assessment' is normally based on something more complex than a strict costs-benefits calculus and those goals that are perceived as important values are sometimes pursued also at very high costs. If the 'self' is constituted by multiple identities and ties, the reductionism of rational choice theory appears weak and unable to explain the reality of the identity-conflict situation.

2.3.2 Plural affiliations and lack of freedoms

Coming back to the PSC theory, the relevant factor in identity-conflicts is due to 'the prolonged and often violent struggle fought by communal groups for such basic needs as security, recognition, and acceptance, fair access to political institutions and economic participation' (Azar 1991: 93). In this framework the role of the state was crucial, because it could satisfy or frustrate such communal human needs, therefore, preventing or promoting conflict. The idea of 'grievances' expressed by supporters of the PSC theory is still crucial for analyzing the identity–violence nexus. To put the PSC theory in contemporary words, it would be possible conceive of the idea of deprivation of fundamental human needs in terms of what Sen has called *capability-deprivation*. This adaptation of the PSC theory is meant to introduce the argument of freedom and the rise of violence resulting from freedom-deprivation. In this perspective, the role of the state is still crucial: the presence of democratic rules able to support individuals' free expression and self-determination represents an important condition for peace within society. In addition, this approach is meant to emphasize the role of individuals with their plural affiliations as the main subject of the analysis, reducing the emphasis on identity groups.

In his development ethics, Sen recovers from the Aristotelian tradition an idea of *functionings* consisting of various doings and being, such as moving around, working, being well nourished, being free of disease, but also subjective states, as being happy, being respected (Sen 1999). Accordingly, a person's state can be defined as a *vector of functionings*; therefore, the person's *capability to function* is represented by the combination of vectors of functioning that are available for him. Sen therefore relates this notion of capabilities to that of substantive freedoms (ibid.: 36). Poverty is therefore understood as resulting from the broader notion of capability-deprivation, since it entails individual deprivations of basic rights and freedoms. Several empirical studies have shown a direct relation between capability-deprivation and violence (Sen 2008).

In the analysis of identity-conflicts, this notion of *capabilities-deprivation* entails four crucial aspects, namely deprivation of political rights and participation, lack of economic opportunities and widespread inequalities, denial of security rights, and lack of recognition intended as constraints to make a free choice regarding the priority to give to the different affiliations. The last point can be understood by considering, for instance, the condition of a Jewish man in the Nazi Germany of the Second World War; undoubtedly, his choice about the priority of his affiliations was deeply limited from the perception that the German people had of him (Sen 2006a). An identity-conflict is therefore more likely to occur if within society there is a widespread condition of *capabilities-deprivation*.

As for the notion of poverty, the idea of *capability-deprivation* takes into account several factors (i.e. economic in-equalities, unfair access to political institutions and denial of political and civil rights, high and unequally distributed levels of illiteracy). Unlike the approach to 'greed vs grievances', this account considers poverty in terms of lack of substantive freedoms. It therefore involves a series of factors that were neglected in the framework proposed by Collier and the scholars of the economic approach. As I have argued with respect to the Bosnian case, in several cases of conflict, poverty, alone, does not offer a convincing explanation for the outbreak of violence. More attention should be paid to the high level of inequalities in rate of illiteracy, access to political institutions, and levels of income between rural and the urban areas, both before and during the war.

In addition, the idea of capability-deprivation entails a special attention to political and civil rights and political participation. The state's failure to guarantee civil and political rights and a fair political participation for all citizens functions as structural pre-condition for conflict. Very often, the demise of totalitarian regimes (as in the case of Bosnia) or emergence of authoritarian rules (as in several cases of conflict in Africa), function as 'accelerator factors', which exacerbate the tensions within society and are likely to lead to the outbreak of violence (Ayoob 1996). In a democratic state, the guarantee of civil and political rights and freedoms, which enable people to lead the lives they want to live, offers a 'detailed and more satisfying substitute' for violence (Barnett 2008: 82). Furthermore, an elected government is less likely to create situations of social grievances and inequalities, because it would lose the support of citizens.[22] Therefore, on the one hand, the lack of civil and political rights and freedoms creates deep divisions between them and the institutions which should guarantee peace and stability. On the other hand, the absence of democratic rules generates social grievances and economic crisis (Sen 1999).

Lastly, the approach rooted in the idea of *capabilities-deprivation* takes into serious consideration the frustration and the sense of deprivation resulting from the lack freedom in expressing or choosing one or more identities over the others. The ethnic or religious heterogeneity does not represent *per se* an obstacle to peace and stability (Sen 2008). Nevertheless, the condition of security is deeply related to the fair access to the institutions of government, to cultural tolerance, and to acceptance of diversity within society. Very often, the deprivation of physical needs and the denial of access to social institutions are deeply linked to the refusal to recognize or accept ethnic or religious affiliations of the others. As I have shown before, the emergence of racial, ethnic or religious violence is often linked to a peculiar understanding of nation as territorially based cultural community. Therefore, the lack of recognition creates social grievances, exclusion and marginalization within society. Society appears to be redesigned in terms of losers and winners, marginalized and not. The sense of frustration resulting from the denial of access to social institutions, is an important motivating factor for social struggles.

To consider again the Bosnian case, practices of 'apartheid', understood as political and economic exclusion, were put into action by representatives of the three groups almost everywhere in the country between the end of the 1980s and the beginning of the 1990s (Kaldor 1999). Furthermore, these practices are still omnipresent in the territory (Flottau and Kraske 2005). Since the end of the war several displaced people have expressed that they are afraid to return home, very often they return only to sell their homes and properties, since in their homeland there is no place for them in terms of economic opportunities and political participation (Kolind 2007).

2.3.3 Value-rationality, 'cultural-war-entrepreneurs' and violence

The grievances resulting from the lack of freedoms and rights produce more or less latent conflicting conditions; but, such a situation, alone, hardly led to the outbreak of war. An identity-conflict occurs when this situation of capability-deprivation is supplemented by the emergence of what I call 'cultural-war-entrepreneurs' (Anheier and Isar 2007). In this last section, I attempt to explain the role played by 'cultural-war-entrepreneurs', such as political, religious or military leaders, but also regular criminals, in deeply divided societies; these actors, usually acting in associations/organizations, fuel violence leading to the outbreak of the conflict. The argument is developed following three key issues. First, in contrast to individualist reductionism, I understand the actions and behaviours of these actors in the light of a broader idea of value-rationality (1). The second issue is concerned with the identification of such 'cultural-war-entrepreneurs' and their relation with identity groups. In this context, the idea of identity-associations, based on an individualistic account, is meant to replace the notion of identity-groups (2). Thus, the third issue concerns the actual impact of these actors in deeply divided societies (3).

(1) Individualist reductionism assumes that individual behaviour in conflict can be explained in terms of rational choice; in such a context, an actor is defined as rational if his actions are aimed at realizing self-interest on the basis of a costs-benefits calculus. In contrast to this view, I argue that, although private interests play a significant role in igniting the conflict and upholding high levels of violence, this can hardly be explained in terms of *instrumental rationality* (Varshney 2003b).

First, scholars of the rational choice theory assume that identity-based argument can be understood as instrumental means used by leaders for manipulating masses (ibid.). However, such a kind of argument, alone, can hardly explain the mobilizing power of identity-based arguments. Even accepting the instrumental-based argument about identity, this cannot explain why leaders should decide to mobilize ethnic or religious passions, rather than other aspects or interests, in order to get power. Varshney offers a clear explanation of this point, 'a purely instrumental conception of ethnicity' he says 'cannot explain why leaders mobilize ethnic or national identities at all'(Varshney 2003b: 89). The point is analogous to Jon Elster's famous objection to the instrumental conception of norms: 'Some argue that... norms... are tools of manipulation, used to dress up self-interest in a more acceptable garb. But this cannot be true.... If some people successfully exploit norms for self-interested purposes, it can only be because others are willing to let norms take precedence over self-interest' (ibid.).

In this perspective, rationality should be interpreted rather as a form of 'reasoned assessment' which is based not only on individual self-interest, but also on general values and beliefs. This is what Varshey calls 'value-rationality' that is the category where many identity-conflicts belong. In this view, religious or ethnic features are understood both as a means to fulfil self-interested ends (e.g. the case of free riders), or as proper group goals or interests, so it is rational to select appropriate means to realize these goals or choosing between competing group goals (Varshney 2003b: 94).

(2) The second issue concerns the identification of the 'cultural-war-entrepreneurs' and their relation with identity groups. In contrast to Azar's idea of identity group as an expression of community values, my second argument offers an explanation of 'cultural-war-entrepreneurs' in terms of associations of individuals that make use of the identity-based argument to follow their own, very often criminal or illegal, interests. Although the condition of capabilities-deprivation of society is seen as the root of the internal conflict, very often associations or groups of individuals make use of the sense of revenge and frustration of people, which becomes a 'public justification' for creating a certain level of support to violent actions. Following Brubaker, it would be possible to look at these actors in terms of 'organizations' of individuals. According to him, in fact, with reference to ethno-religious groups it might be useful to make a distinction between groups as category and groups as organizations (Brubaker 2004). Thus, he argues that 'although participants' rhetoric and commonsense accounts treat ethnic groups as the protagonists of most ethnic conflict, in fact the chief protagonist of most ethnic [...] violence are not groups as such but various kind of organizations' (ibid.: 41).

Such a distinction between groups and organizations can be useful to trace a clear difference between the quest of recognition and free choice among the identitarian attributions of individuals within society and the use that 'cultural-war-entrepreneurs' can make of such a quest. The demagogic use of the identity-based

arguments depends, on the one hand, on the thuggish interests and grim purposes of these individuals that find convenience in manipulating the masses to
lead to the outbreak of violence, and on the other, on the weakness of the individuals within society. This weakness can be understood as an effect of the practices of misrecognition discussed in the previous section. These practices, such
as apartheid, economic exclusion, or political segregation, lead to the denial of
the individual freedom to select and give priority to certain affiliations over the
others. This imprisons individuals to recognize themselves in the way in which
other groups look at them; and, therefore, they lose their own identity and personal experiences.

(3) The last issue relates to the emergence of the earlier-mentioned 'cultural-war-entrepreneurs' and the development of the warfare. To refer to Kalyvas's
argument, it is possible to understand internal conflicts in the light of the interaction
between Hobbes's view of conflict, as linked to private interest and actions of individuals, and Rousseau's conception of 'public interest'. In such a frame, in fact,
cultural-war-entrepreneurs manipulate master cleavages, based on religious or ethnic arguments, making use of a dialectic based on the idea of 'public interests'
of their community (Kalyvas 2003). In other terms, a combination of two kinds
of warfare is recognizable in identity-conflicts. On the one hand, an individual-
based 'war of all against all' (ibid.: 475) emerges; in such a context, cultural-
war-entrepreneurs are meant to be a variety of individuals that, with various ti-
tles, are involved in violent actions, rather than elites that rationally manipulate
masses. On the other, Rousseau's idea of 'public interest' suggests an understanding
of war as 'state to state'. To be more precise, in the case of identity-conflicts we
can refer to 'community to community', where the role of the 'cultural-war-
entrepreneurs', understood as elites, seems to be more relevant. Once again, it
is important to emphasize that this 'second side' of warfare is linked to three factors deeply related to each other: the role of the elites, the effects of capability-
deprivation on societies, and the historical development of a cultural-based idea
of nation.

This logic of warfare is not only responsible for the outbreak of violence, but
it fuels a condition for a protracted conflict within society. The combination of
the two kinds of warfare creates new local powers based on an idea of biological
supremacy — often articulated in terms of race, language or ethno-religious features — which Foucault would have called 'bio-power', able to protract the condition of war in situations of 'alleged peace'. This perspective reverses the Clausewitzean understanding of war, since it introduces Foucault's idea that in such deeply
divided societies the so-called 'peace' is a 'continuation of war by other means'
(Foucault 2003). The case of contemporary Bosnia offers several examples of how

such a process of 'continuation of war by other means' works in a transitional society. Although the levels of violence in the region are decreased after the 'formal' end of the war, there are still situations of ethno-religious segregation and exclusion in several cities (ICG 2002b). Furthermore, typical of this condition of 'protracted conflict' is the lack of an approach aiming at a genuine reconciliation, in other terms able to relate peace to justice indissolubly. In Bosnia, today, most of the war criminals are still at large; very often, they are protected by the respective nationalist political parties (ICG 2000; Delpla 2007).[23]

64

NOTESNOTES

1. For an interesting discussion on the characteristics of deeply divided societies see also Guelke (2012).

2. I am referring to the recent interventions in Bosnia, Rwanda, Somalia, East Timor and Kosovo. When I use the term 'intervention', I am not referring to the actual intervention to bring to an end the hostilities. My idea of 'intervention' entails rather the notion of 'conflict transformation'. In literature, one can distinguish three different approaches to conflicts: conflict management (1), conflict resolution (2), and conflict transformation (3):

   (1) The first approach is a 'realist approach' and it is focused on the management of violence (Pia and Diez 2007). (2) Conflict resolution theorists look at the deep-rooted sources of the conflict in order to offer non-coercive and informal solutions that can involve controlled communication, problem-solving workshops or round tables (Fetherston 1999). (3) The last approach can be seen as the deepest level of conflict resolution tradition (Ramsbotham et al. 2006). According to conflict transformation theorists, 'conflict transformation must actively envision, include, respect, and promote the human and cultural resources from within a giving setting. This involves a new set of lenses through which we do

not primarily, "see" the setting and the people in it as the problem and the outsider as the answer' (Lederach 1995: 212).

3. Clausewitz (1989: book I, chapter 2 titled 'Ends and Means in War'): '[...] If, in the next place, we keep once more to the pure conception of war, then we must say that its political object properly lies out of its province, for if war is an act of violence to compel the enemy to fulfil our will, then in every case all depends on our overthrowing the enemy, that is, disarming him, and on that alone. This object, developed from abstract conceptions, but which is also the one aimed at in a great many cases in reality, we shall, in the first place, examine in this reality [...].'

4. It is necessary to clarify that this distinction does not include all the theories existing about ethnic conflicts. I am adopting explanatory categories. In particular, the usage of the categories of statism and cosmopolitanism is meant to link primordialist and constructive perspectives to the phenomenon of globalization. Actually, the main difference between these authors is linked to their answers to globalization rather than to their perspectives regarding the cultural dimension of such conflicts. The primordialist or constructivist standpoints, in fact, seem to be functional arguments for supporting their views regarding the

future of world politics in a globalized age.

5. Western, Confucian, Japanese, Islamic, Hindu, Slavic-Orthodox, Latin American and African civilizations.

6. I am referring here to the title of Kalyvas's (2001) article '"New" and "Old" Civil Wars: A Valid Distinction?'

7. In contrast to the well-known levels of analysis framework proposed by Kenneth Waltz, in which he distinguished system, state and individual levels.

8. He defined cultural violence as 'those aspects of culture that can be used to justify or legitimize direct or structural violence' (Galtung 1990: 291).

9. I am quoting here Horowitz (1998: premise).

10. Regarding the usage of these two kinds of reductionism see also Sen (2006a).

11. Another interesting view of the idea of identity, based on an idea of identifications, is presented by Maffettone (2006a) in his essay, 'Psiche e Polis').

12. E. Renan, 'Qu'estce qu'une nation?' (in Hutchinson and Smith 1994: 18).

13. M. Weber, 'The Nation' (in Hutchinson and Smith 1994: 25).

14. J. Stalin, 'The Nation' (in Hutchinson and Smith 1994: 20).

15. I am considering the cases of India, South Africa, Senegal, Cameroun, to mention only a few.

16. During the interview with Mehmed Musić, the president of the association of victims of the municipality of Hadžići, he reported the actual involvement of an orthodox bishop named Milan Lucic in the activities of ethnic cleansing in that zone. Sarajevo, 30 November 2007.

17. Several authors used to make a distinction between 'religion' and 'religious background', stressing in this way how the religious content of the three religious faiths had been harmonized over the centuries within the boundaries of a shared Bosnian culture; see also Donia and Fine (1994).

18. Low per capita income is interpreted as an indicator able to demonstrate the incapacity of the state to maintain effective control over its territory (Fearon and Laitin 2003). Both low income and slow growth are interpreted as lowering the recruitment cost of rebel troops, and the predation of natural resources can provide rebel organizations with finance. Lastly, the control over the exports of natural resources (diamonds, drugs, or oil) is considered as a factor that can activate private interests in conflict.

19. According to Mary Kaldor (1999), in December 1989 the monthly inflation rate reached 2,500 per cent.

20. See in this respect chapter 4 on the Bosnian case study.

21. Interview with Ema Čekić, president of the Association for the Missing Persons of the Vogošća Municipality, Sarajevo, 2 December 2007.

22. In this respect, see also Sen's argument about the role of democracy in preventing famine, 'Famine and Other Crises' (Sen 1999: 161–87).

23. I will discuss these issues related to the case of Bosnia in the chapter 4.

Chapter 3

From conflict to civil society: a normative perspective

3.1 Understanding civil society: history and possibilities – 3.2 Contemporary revival of civil society – 3.3 A normative proposal for civil society – 3.4 Civil society engagement in deeply divided societies: a theoretical framework – 3.5 Civil society and democratic transition: the idea of 'culture of civility'

Recently, much scholarly work has put emphasis on the constructive potential of civil society in the processes of conflict transformation and democratic transition. Increasingly, both academics and practitioners have drawn attention to the positive role of Civil Society Organizations (CSOs) not only with reference to track one, the so-called humanitarian intervention, but also with reference to the impact of these associations in the so-called track two, the post-conflict phase (Aall 2001; Orjuela 2003; Ramsbotham 2005; Ramsbotham et al. 2006). In addition to the support offered to civilians in wartime, NGOs, and, more in general, CSOs are supposed to play a positive role in supporting post-conflict negotiations and settlements and in endorsing a sustainable reconciliation among former fighting groups (Rupesinghe 1998). In particular, supporters of civil society engagement in conflict transformation have stressed the peculiar role of civil society actors in deeply divided societies (Fetherston, 1999; Kaldor, 2003a; Varshney, 2001, 2003a). After an identity-conflict, civil society is generally perceived as the space where it is possible to reconcile and balance individual autonomy and collective aspirations and claims. Civil society is therefore supposed to function as the 'good society' able to 'civilize' the context of war, shaping the basis for pluralistic and modern democracy (Belloni 2001).

However, the perspectives about civil society engagement in divided societies vary deeply with respect to two key issues, the interpretation of identity-conflicts, and the very idea of civil society. As I noted in the previous chapter, different understandings of collective identity are likely to lead to different understandings of these conflicts. I have distinguished two extreme perspectives: the culturalist and the rational choice approach to conflicts and, therefore, identified these approaches in terms of cultural and individualist reductionism. In the last section, I have emphasized the urgency to consider those conflicts in the light of an understanding of individuals' actions and motivations in the light of their multiple identities.

This chapter is instead focused on the notion of civil society and its impact on conflict transformation and democratic transition of deeply divided societies. It comprises two sections. The first is devoted to a deeper understanding of the notion of civil society in the light of an account of its traditional understanding in Western political thought and an analysis of three contemporary approaches in the different fields of political science, post-colonial studies, and international relations theories. Thus, in the next section, the analysis of the Western liberal tradition referring to the notion of civil society is meant to emphasize the central role played by 'freedom', understood as the major feature of the notion of civil society. In this context, I distinguish three different streams. The FS stream, which recovers what I call the counter-absolutist tradition, and places civil society in the private sphere. The PS stream emphasizes the eminently political role of civil society. Finally, the G stream relates civil society to the cultural domain. Accordingly, these streams are adapted to the present revival of civil society. I analyze three contemporary approaches emerging from different fields and, finally, following Hegel's scheme, I introduce a more complex notion of civil society.

The second section is therefore focused on the analysis of the impact of civil society in deeply divided societies. In this part, again the emphasis is placed on the idea of individual identity and its impact on the idea of civil society in identity-conflicts. I offer a literary review of contemporary approaches to civil society's engagement in deeply divided societies. In literature, two kinds of reductionism are applied to the concept of identity. These different understandings of identity suggest two distinct ways to look at civil society. Again, cultural reductionism emphasizes the role of groups/communities as a main unit of analysis of those conflicts; and, for this reason, civil society is seen as that sphere where these conflicts can be handled through the mutual recognition of such groups/communities. In this perspective, civil society is understood as a kind of 'anticipation' of the more extensive experience of the state. On the contrary, individualist reductionism suggests that individuals' interests and actions are at the roots of violence. In this context, civil society has to be seen as a kind of antistate: that space, independent from the state, where individual autonomy is realized and universal values are fostered.

In this book a third view is suggested, civil society is both a kind of 'antici-pation' of the more extensive experience of the state and a counterweight to state power. Civil society associations and movements are the locus where what I call the 'culture of civility' emerges and is nurtured. This culture can be understood as a kind of non-institutional consensus on a specific tradition of civility, made up of shared values and traditions, which enables individuals to become part of a community of citizens and accept to reciprocate and give reasonably acceptable reasons based on the overall acceptance of some universal values, such as con-demnation of racist regimes or respect of human dignity. In essence, the idea of a culture of civility aims at addressing both justice and a kind of stability for the 'right reasons' in the process of transition of divided societies.

According to the definition provided by the Centre for Civil Society of the London School of Economics:

> [...] Civil society refers to the arena of un-coerced collec-tive action around shared interests, purposes and values. In theory, its institutional forms are distinct from those of the state, family and market, though in practice, *the boundaries between state, civil society, family and market are often complex, blurred and negotiated.*[1] [Emphasis added]

Actually, in spite of its centrality to Western political thought, there is an overall disagreement over the content and the extent of civil society, both in theoretical and empirical terms. In literature, one can discover a huge variety of meanings assigned to civil society in history (Edwards 2004). In some cases it is defined as 'the nature of good society', while, in other contexts, civil society is supposed to represent either a way to live together peacefully through the reconciliation of individual autonomy with collective aspirations or a means for balancing freedom and its boundaries.

Thus, although it is popular across societies of different levels and across all ideological hues, the idea of civil society seems to be confused and confusing. In order to reconstruct the content of this notion and its evolution in contemporary literature I propose to analyze civil society from the point of view of the most relevant aspect involved in it. In Western political theory, in fact, the debate about civil society has been constructed around a fundamental political issue concerning the role of freedom in the political realm. Whatever have been the approaches to society, and its relations to political, cultural and economic implications, the links between public and private as well as between public ethics and individual interests have represented key features of modern political thought (Seligman 1992). In philosophical debate, it is possible to recognize three different streams that have related the notion of civil society and the issue of freedom to the three different domains of culture, economy and politics.

Today, we are facing a revival of the concept of civil society. Such a revival is mostly due to the emergence of new actors and movements that have increasingly captured the attention of scholars and practitioners. Religious and ethnical movements and associations, NGOs and no-profit organizations, social movements and groups of activists, represent the renewed expression of civil society. Recently, the notion of civil society has been recovered from political philosophy and applied to other scholarly fields. In the contemporary usage, the three streams translate into three different approaches to civil society. First, a 'post-colonial' version is likely to recognize in the notion of civil society elements which are rooted in modern Western culture and traditions. Second, a 'neo-liberal' approach, rooted in the Scottish Enlightened tradition and enriched by Tocqueville's reminiscences, has recovered an idea of civil society as a kind of private sphere quite distinct from the state structure. Finally, a new political account, with a quite evident cosmopolitan trend, has emerged in Western Europe. This last account is likely to reconcile the traditional idea of an existing close link between civil society and deliberative democracy with a transnational idea of justice 'beyond territorial borders'.

3.1.1 Civil society as counter-absolutist argument

Despite the presence of significantly new factors, the present revival of civil society introduces some important features of continuity with the Western political philosophical tradition. In particular, despite the differences of view, the notion of civil society has been associated to the realization of freedom related to the enquiry about society.

The first context where it is possible to recognize an original idea of civil society seems to be the ancient Greek political thought.[2] Aristotle defined man as the political animal (ζοών πολιτικόν = *zoon politicon*) and *polis* (πόλις) as the most perfect form in which this natural *telos* (τέλος) of the human beings could have been realized. In this context, the notion of political community (πολιτικόν κοινονήμα = politicon koinonema) represented a close equivalent of the Latin *societas civilis*. With this expression Greeks, and later Romans, used to define the virtue implicit in law-governed societies, as a locus of public goods. In these societies, freedom was fully realized in the public sphere (πολιτεία = *politeia*).[3] The *polis*, as well as later the Roman Empire, was the level where the 'public good' was achieved, the *civility* of society was therefore defined by its political and public organization.[4]

This way of interpreting civil society came back into use when philosophers began to contemplate the foundation of the emerging absolute states (Taylor 1995). First, Thomas Hobbes formulated his idea of *civil society* in terms of Commonwealth (hereafter, political society). The constitution of Hobbes's political society was due to people's acceptance, by virtue of the *pactum subjectionis* (contract of subjection), to be governed by an absolute king. This scheme was meant to justify a rights-based society, founded on the contract, which would have replaced the 'state of nature', where the life of man was solitary, poor, nasty and violent. According to Hobbes, by accepting to live in a civil society people were required to abandon the condition of freedom, which constituted a key human attribution in the 'state of nature'.[5]

The reason for this distinction between a 'free state of nature' and a 'safe civil society governed by an absolute king' can be easily understood in the light of an analysis of the historical context. Actually, since the early Middle Ages, a notion of (civil) society, where political authority was *singulis maior sed universalis minor* (one organ among others), was developed. The first relevant attempt to differentiate an idea of community/society from the political organization was made by the Church. Actually, the crucial feature of Latin Christendom was represented by the assumption that postulated the separation between temporal and spiritual powers/societies; in this context the Church was supposed to be an independent society.[6]

Then, the communal organization of the state in the late Middle Ages constituted a further development in this sense. A typical example of the medieval structure of power presented a sort of diarchy that ensured relative freedom for its subjects: a monarch, who embodied the idea of central power, was supposed to govern vast territories, but several cities/territorial authorities upheld a relatively independent administrative and bureaucratic system. The idea of sovereignty developed by Hobbes may therefore be understood as a way to undermine the medieval mixed system of power. The space for freedom and self-government needed to be replaced by the absolute regime.

However, after Hobbes, the notion of civil society, understood as a realm distinct from the political organization, became a fundamental argument of the counter-absolutist thinkers (Taylor 1995). Locke offered the first version of this kind of view. Although he was still referring to an idea of political society, Locke introduced two relevant features: the first related to the 'state of nature' and the second to the idea of contract. The 'state of nature', in Locke, was characterized by an embryonic notion of 'humankind' as a pre-political community, where the respect for others was supposed to compensate both for freedom and for self-interest.[7] Instead of 'a state of war', it was related to a state of economic progress, where private property emerged and developed.[8] Locke's idea of contract is also quite peculiar since it introduces an important idea of a fiduciary relationship between the government and the governed. Since a (civil) society already existed by virtue of an original contract (*pactum unionis*) by which men agreed to live under a legal system which would protect their natural rights, the second contract (*pactum sub-*

jectionis) implied that members of the society accepted to be governed by a particular form of government on the basis of a fiduciary relationship.

Thus, even presenting elements of the ancient tradition, Locke opened the channels for a revival of society as the *locus* of freedom. Two important implications followed from his work. First, new relevance was being given to economic progress (capitalism), seen as the basis for a new individualism and a rights-based society. Second, individuals organized in a society were supposed to determine, or at least influence, the course of state policy. However, a clear distinction between civil society and political society was formulated only years later, due to the contribution of the Scottish Enlightenment first, and then Hegel and Tocqueville.

The idea of civil society articulated by Ferguson and Smith upheld and developed Locke's intuitions about both relevance and autonomy of the economic sphere. Both authors elaborated a picture of society as an economy; that is, the domain of the private sphere. In this context, the content of such economy was closely linked with the Aristotelian idea of oikonomia (οἰκονομία = household law). These authors conceived of civil society as a kind of natural order due to the division of labour. It was the realm of freedom thought in opposition to the artificial order of the state.[9] A further feature of differentiation between the Scottish Enlightenment and the Lockean perspective was related to the moral nature of civil society. Both Smith and Ferguson wanted to break with the ancient contractarian tradition that linked such a morality to the subordination of humans to God.[10] Conversely, for Ferguson and Smith the source of morality of civil society had to be found in those 'moral sentiments' and 'natural benevolence' that characterized the human world. They used the definition of 'moral greed' as an attempt to distinguish a kind of reasonable self-interest free of 'passions' and morally bounded from a mere idea of rationality (Seligman 2002).

3.1.2 Civil society as democratic expedient: from Tocqueville to the public sphere

Starting from the twentieth century, a controversy between liberals and communitarians has emerged with reference to civil society. Again, at the centre of this debate has been a fundamental political issue concerning freedom. In this context, the idea of civil society has assumed different connotations, depending on whether the idea of freedom should have been explained in the light of individual rights or of the community's shared norms.

On the one hand, a Kantian liberal view has considered the respect for individual rights and the principle of political neutrality as the paradigm for legitimacy in constitutional democracy. According to this view, individuals own moral rights that would serve as constraints on government. These rights are considered not on the ground of some social convention but by virtue of their having some 'property' – moral autonomy, human dignity, etc. – that constitutes them as bearers of rights. On the other hand, the communitarian critique of the rights thesis has focused on its individualist assumptions and universalistic claims. According to them, individuals are embedded in a historical and social context; this means that they derive their individual and collective identity from the community. Thus, it is possible to speak about a priority of the context over the individual.

The scholars of the public sphere seek to offer a synthesis between the views of liberals and communitarians. The notion of public sphere occupies an important position in contemporary debate about civil society. Theorists of the public sphere – to quote only few names, Jurgen Habermas, Jean Cohen and Andrew Arato – have looked at civil society as a 'democratic expedient'. According to them,

> Modern civil societies are characterized by a plurality of form of life, they are structurally differentiated and socially heterogeneous. [...] Thus, to be able to lead a moral life, individual autonomy and individual right must be secured. In this view, *it is democracy, with its emphasis on consensus, or at least on majority rule, that is dangerous to liberty*, unless suitably restricted by constitutionally guaranteed basic rights (Cohen and Arato 1994: 10).

Before them, in the Western tradition, Tocqueville's work on democracy in the US played a pivotal role in showing the existing link between modern democracy and civil society (Tocqueville 1840). In particular, he argued that the proliferation of free associations, spontaneously formed by people for the achievement of common purposes out of the state, was alleged to be the only guarantee against the tyranny of the majority's rule. With Tocqueville, the spirit of voluntary associations became a crucial aspect of the idea of civil society. In his view, civil society became a 'democratic expedient' that enabled people to avoid despotism and protect individual freedom.

The core idea of Tocqueville's analysis was characterized by the priority given to free and voluntary associations in the public space. Tocqueville looked at the existence of an active voluntary sector as the necessary condition to balance the centralized power of the state. Although he did not use the term civil society, he assumed a close connection between the existence of a self-regulated and autonomous public sphere and democracy. In this context, his argument about the value of 'associational life' has represented a central issue in systematic studies on the alleged link between democracy and public space.[11]

Contemporary theorists of the public sphere see civil society as the setting for the associational life of individuals. Governed by the rule of law, the public sphere is alleged to sustain the formation of 'public opinion', which represents a crucial tool for bringing the state under control. The rejection of the Hegelian position is at stake in this notion of civil society.[12] In the first instance, in contrast with the counter-absolutist tradition, they reject the idea of civil society as a realm of private interests distinct from the public political space.

> [...] Only a concept of civil society that is properly differentiated from the economy [...] could become the centre of a critical political and social theory in society where the market economy has already developed [...] its autonomous logic (Cohen and Arato 1994: 8).

Accordingly, they challenge the dialectical division of social space into civil society versus external state. These scholars are actually likely to emphasize that the historical changes that occurred in contemporary Western societies (media developments, the science of public opinion engineering, etc.) have altered the possibility to easily distinguish the state from the private level.

Thus, they conceive of civil society as a 'sphere of social interaction between economy and state' (Cohen and Arato 1994: 9). They include in the general notion of public sphere above all the intimate sphere (family), the sphere of associations (in particular, voluntary associations) social movements and forms of public communication (media in general). The public sphere functions as the communicative structure of reference of civil society. Plurality, publicity, privacy and legality are all main attributions of this normative notion of civil society. In particular, they emphasize the necessity of the inclusion of legality, understood as system of rights, in civil society. These rights are meant to protect the inviolability of the private sphere and the effective participation of citizens.

In this account, civil society plays a key role in the democratic procedure. It represents the substratum for an autonomous public sphere, which corresponds to one of the most important guarantees for a vibrant and reliable democracy. The public sphere is where people can discuss matters of mutual concern, and learn about facts, events, opinions, interests and perspectives of others. Discourses on values, norms, laws and policies generate a politically informed public opinion. Public opinion is supposed to influence the debates within political institutions. It brings under informal control the actions and decisions of rulers and lawmakers. This perspective implies that openness of access and parity of participation (equal voice) are those ideals required for the democratic legitimacy of any institutional arrangement.

3.1.3 Civil society and cultural direction

Further developments of the notion of freedom, implicit in the conception of civil society, led to an idea of civil society as a means of contestation against state power. The core idea of this anti-political notion of civil society was already present in the idea of 'right to rebellion' that Locke assigned to society.

Locke considered the political structure as an emanation of the society. It, in turn, was seen as already political, because, by virtue of a first contract, people had put in common their power to enforce the Law of Nature, though they did not have yet an institutional system of power. In this scheme, a prepolitical life was distinguished from the unity of political society. The government represented a further level. Actually, political structures derived from a free choice of the society, and it was meant as guarantee for the safety of the citizens. Nevertheless, such a society maintained the right and power to make and unmake the government. This right was supposed to play a crucial role if government would have failed to serve its mandate. According to Locke, government could have been dissolved when the legislative would have violated the trust placed in it by citizens. The violation of the mandate by the government led to its dissolution and restored the original right of people to determine their political structures. In this context, 'a right to rebellion' enabled people to resist any further governmental effort to exert its power.[13]

Locke's idea of a 'right to rebellion' introduces a notion of society as a means to preserve the power of government or, vice versa, to resist it. In a different vein, Gramsci is the author that has better synthesized this idea of civil society, as the ground for consensus or contestation (Gramsci 1910–26). In this perspective, civil society had such a double function. On the one hand, it was understood as the realm of the morals and culture on which the existing order is grounded. On the other hand, it upheld a relative autonomy and priority over the state, so it was also seen as the sphere on which a new social order could be founded. Gramsci placed a strong emphasis on this emancipatory potential of civil society. It was supposed to function as an agent of stabilization when it was in agreement with the political structure; but it was likely to become an agent of transformation when it represented interests and values conflicting with the constituted power.

Civil society consisted of a wide range of social and cultural interactions, which constituted a kind of wedge between state and class-structured economy. This notion of civil society recovered the Hegelian perspective rather than the Marxian one. Thus, in opposition to the Marxian assumption of bourgeois society as part of the economic structure, the Italian theorist placed civil society in the superstructure, along with the state. As did Hegel, Gramsci assigned to civil society a crucial role: it represented the ethical content of the state (Bobbio 1988). A state without civil society was a *dominio* without hegemony, that is, a dictatorship (Bates 1975).

However, a further feature was related to the role of culture and intellectuals. For Gramsci, the family was included in civil society, since he saw this institution as central in shaping the general political dispositions of citizens. The family was supposed to spread culture and thus hegemony (see also Chambers 2002). Accordingly, civil society was understood as an ethical political moment, independent from political society. In such a context, the notion of ideology, understood as the primary moment of history, played a crucial role. It was related to the moment of cultural direction: a strong ideology was needed for cultural direction. In Gramsci's understanding, cultural direction, which implied an intellectual and moral reform, was supposed to be crucial for hegemony. Thus, the political direction, peculiar of the political structure, without a strong cultural direction was a *dominio* without hegemony.

In this sense, a strong ideology was alleged to be a means to resist and subvert the established order. Studying the Italian case Gramsci emphasized that in the struggle against fascism the Italian Communist Party had to gain positions in civil society for challenging the hegemony of the bourgeoisie. He saw the revolutionary potential of civil society for dislodging the bourgeoisie. Thus, he was suggesting an idea of civil society able to create a strong counter-hegemony. As Cox (1999: 25) has argued, 'the concept of civil society in this emancipatory sense designates the combination of forces upon which the support for a new state and a new order can be built'. Thus, in the light of this conception of hegemony, it is possible to conclude that freedom was realized in the political realm when civil society was consistent with political society.

To conclude this brief theoretical account, one can argue that the distinction between civil society and state has held a pivotal position in Western political thought as an argument in defense of freedom, whether public or private. In the light of such a review, it is possible to distinguish three streams that are deeply influencing contemporary literature on civil society.

i First, following Lockean intuitions about the relevance of the autonomy of the economic sphere, a stream emerges from the Scottish thinkers (hereafter FS stream). The FS stream played a crucial role as a counter-absolutist argument and became a necessary argument in defence of private freedom. It looked at the economy as an autonomous sphere where human morality emerged. As rightly emphasized by Seligman, such an 'economy' has not to be understood as a neutral arena of exchange, it has rather to be seen as a moral sphere, which drew its morality from the moral nature of man himself (Seligman 2002).

ii   Second, in the light of Tocqueville's contribution to the idea of civil society as 'democratic expedient', a public sphere stream (hereafter PS stream) has looked at civil society as a tool of stabilization of democratic regimes. In this stream, civil society is supposed to be a 'democratic expedient' in a specific way, since it is considered as the structure on which the public sphere stands. In turn, the public sphere is characterized by the emergence of the 'public opinion': a notion that recovers the content of the Kantian idea of publicity (Habermas 1989) which is supposed to modify or, at least, correct the democratic directions of politics.

iii Finally, starting from the idea of the ethical content of civil society as distinct from the state, an idea of civil society of an anti-political kind has been developed mostly by the Italian philosopher Antonio Gramsci. This stream (hereafter G stream) places civil society in the cultural domain and introduces its counter-hegemonic potential. In this context, the realization of freedom in civil society is due to its capacity to become a means of rebellion or, at least, contestation against the state. Thus, the emergence of a dominant culture, understood as a tool for a counte-hegemonic power, is emphasized.

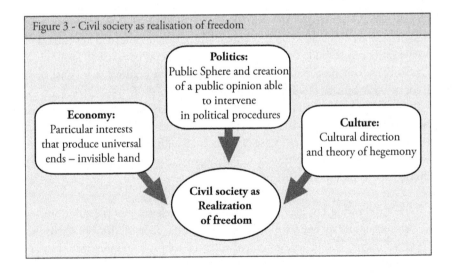

Figure 3 - Civil society as realisation of freedom

Politics:
Public Sphere and creation of a public opinion able to intervene in political procedures

Economy:
Particular interests that produce universal ends – invisible hand

Culture:
Cultural direction and theory of hegemony

Civil society as Realization of freedom

3.2
CONTEMPORARY REVIVAL OF CIVIL SOCIETY

In recent years, the emergence of many different non-state actors has emphasized the necessity to pay new attention to civil society. Religious and ethnic movements, non-governmental organizations, and social movements represent the renewed expressions of civil society. The new content of civil society reflects the profound changes that have intervened, during the last two decades, in the categories of politics, economy and culture. In this perspective, the present renaissance of civil society suggests not only a kind of continuity of the emerging political paradigm with fundamental tendencies of modernity, but it also refers to something significantly new (Cohen and Arato 1994).

Actually, if it is true that contemporary formulations of civil society reflect the relevance of the modern Western tradition, however, contemporary scholars, from different fields and disciplines, are increasingly enriching this notion of new contents in order to adapt it to the new paradigms of the 'post-national era'. Thus, the idea of freedom and the possibilities for its realization into the political realm represent once again the crucial issues at stake. Furthermore, the streams listed in the previous section influence contemporary notions and approaches to civil society, considered in turn as the domain of culture, economy, or politics. It is possible to summarize at least three different approaches to civil society. Each approach considers one side of the phenomenon as basis for further investigations. Following the G stream, the first approach entails a post-colonial perspective that debates civil society from cultural perspective. Therefore, supporters of the FS stream have offered a version of civil society as the realm of the social economy, understood as a third sphere between state and economy (Khilnani 2001; Kaldor 2003a). Finally, the PS stream has been further developed into a political approach to civil society, characterized by a quite evident cosmopolitan trend.

A brief description of the main instances proposed by the three approaches is proposed. In the next section, an inclusive understanding of civil society able to include political economic and cultural features is suggested.

3.2.1 Post-colonial approach to civil society

The 'post-colonial' approach upholds and develops a notion of civil society as understood in the G stream. The supporters of this stream emphasize the limits of a Western-oriented notion of civil society, as postulated by the modern thinkers Locke, Ferguson, Smith and Hegel. Civil society, outside the West, cannot be easily identified with a sphere of private interests and individual freedom based on voluntary and autonomous associations. Only in a few big cities is it possible to identify a sphere of civil society as conceived in the Western tradition (Mamdani 1996). In general, in these contexts, liberal institutions are simply a kind of export of the colonial age that lack those pluralistic forms that are attributions of civil society in the West; thus the question arises whether associational forms exist outside the Western tradition which can fulfil this role.

Post-colonial scholars offer two kinds of answers to the dilemma of the possibility of a kind of non-Western civil society. The main difference between these two approaches is that while a first group of scholars seeks to offer alternative non-Western versions of civil society, a second group of scholars tends to reduce the universality of civil society, which is considered as a phenomenon deeply rooted in Western culture and history. In general, this second group of scholars focuses on a criticism of 'civil society' as a tool of cultural and political domination (Chatterjee 2001).

Conversely, in its first version, the post-colonial myth of civil society assumes new connotations and nuances, and it leads post-colonial scholars to discover 'a chronologic epic of ideas and authors' of a purely non-Western civil society (Comaroff and Comaroff 1999). According to this approach, following the G stream's main assumption about the role of culture in constructing a collective identity and consensus, a counter-hegemonic, and thus post-colonial, version of civil society has emerged. Despite the differences among the cultural backgrounds of the authors, this 'cultural sensitive' idea of civil society would represent an alternative to Western theorizations. Most of these scholars consider the existence of traditional groups and organizations, based on religion, ethnicity, or kinship, as an alternative public space. In this context, instead of notions such as voluntarism and autonomy the ascriptive criteria of kinship or religion are applied (Comaroff and Comaroff 1999; Obadare 2004) producing an 'odd mixture of communitarian corporatism and libertarianism' (Zubaida 2001: 238).

The condition for maintaining the existence of this public space is due to the inclusion of the tolerance. In this context, many scholars refer to the model of the Ottoman Empire and its 'Millet system' as an example of the inclusion of tolerance in a multicultural society. A way in which tolerance can be realized in the public space is through the effort of public intellectuals. Many scholars, arguing the post-colonial version of civil society, entrust a relevant role to intellectuals (Arkoun 2002). As for the G stream, intellectuals with their critical function should offer a direction to political, religious and ethical issues within and beyond national frontiers. According to some scholars, their role is fundamental not only in order to challenge the abuse of power, but also in order to offer a more tolerant interpretation of religious, cultural and moral precepts.

3.2.2 Neo-liberal approach to civil society

The second approach to civil society, neo-liberalism, can be understood in the light of the FS stream. Political scientists and sociologists have developed such a version by taking US's system as a model, during the last two decades. They emphasize the relevance of an emerging 'third sector', distinct from both state and market, in the structure of contemporary democratic states. Nevertheless, they stress the role of such a sector in providing social benefits (Anheier 2000; Fukuyama 1999; Putnam 1995; Putnam and Pharr 2000; Kendall and Knapp 2000).

In this perspective, the emerging non-profit sector can be described as a 'laissez-faire politics', a sort of market in politics (Kaldor 2002, 2003a). The core idea is to consider the emergence of a strong voluntary non-profit sector as a way for creating comparative advantages for the other sectors, such as market and state. On the one hand, a neo-liberal perspective of minimizing the role of state in order to have more efficiency in the market has emerged. On the other, this approach recovers Tocqueville's intuition about the fundamental link between an existing strong associational and voluntary sector and the democratic functioning of contemporary states. Rather than an isolated phenomenon floating freely in social space the 'third sector' is seen as a fundamental part of the social system of reference, linked to both economic and political dynamics.

Related to the notion of 'third sector', the idea of social capital plays a crucial role in this literature. According to Putnam, it is possible to consider social capital as 'features of social organization such as networks, norms, social trust that facilitate coordination and motivation for mutual benefit' (Putnam 1995: 67). Social capital is conceived as the economic and social outcome of the third sector, the sector of the relational networks. As Putnam and Fukuyama have argued, social capital encourages the emergence of social trust, which represents a fundamental resource for modern liberal democracies for two reasons. First, it strongly influences the quality of public life and the performance of the social institutions. Second, it is a crucial element in order to improve the efficiency of the market, through the reduction of the transaction costs associated with formal association mechanisms.

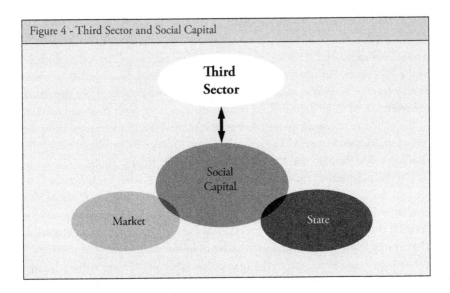

Figure 4 - Third Sector and Social Capital

3.2.3 Cosmopolitan approach to civil society

A last emerging version of civil society is what I define as 'cosmopolitan approach'. This approach has recently been developed by some European scholars, most of them from departments of international relations in the United Kingdom. It combines features of political theory with international relations theories. In this third understanding, the new idea of civil society appears to be connected to the political sphere. In a context in which nation-states do not any longer have the authority to defend their citizens, new civil society movements and organizations would represent a sort of interface between the individual level and the state level (Kaldor 2003b; Keane 2003).

In this perspective, the current renaissance of civil society represents a new crucial political paradigm (Falk 1995, 2002; Kaldor 2002). They date back this revival to the democratic transitions of the 1980s in Eastern Europe and Latin America (Huntington 1991; Kaldor, 2002, 2003a, 2003b; Kaldor and Muro 2003; Keck and Sikkink 1998). In these two regions, the democratic transition was characterized by the emergence of a new type of social movements and non-governmental organizations. In both cases, civil society was a kind of 'war society' (Kaldor 2003b: 586) fighting against two different enemies, totalitarianism in Europe and military dictatorships in Latin America. Although there was no communication between them, these movements waged a war against the regimes emphasizing their autonomy and their civic efforts to create 'islands of civic engagement' (ibid.).

Their new strategy of struggle was based on new values: peaceful opposition and human rights protection. Civil society, in this perspective, implies pluralism, mutual trust, solidarity and cooperation, but moreover it can provide a framework within which the resistance of the individual against the state can be mobilized.

Following the PS stream, such an approach involves a notion of civil society eminently political. In this perspective, civil society has a normative content; it is conceived as a project to be realized at a global level. Global civil society has become the paradigm for a new approach to politics in the post-Westphalian era. New non-state and border-free expressions of political community challenge territorial sovereignty as the exclusive basis for political community and identity. In this perspective, liberal theorists, varying from evident cosmopolitan perspectives (Habermas 2001; Kaldor 2003a, 2002; Held 1995) to more sceptical communitarian positions (Frost 2002; Walzer 1995), conceive of Global Civil Society as an ethical category that should be promoted and fostered on a global scale.

The global reproduction of civil society is understood as able to provide the agency necessary for the democratization of the institutions at the global level. It embodies the liberal values in the transnational dimension:

> global civil society [...] is about 'civilizing' or democratizing globalization, about the process through which groups, movements and individuals can demand a global rule of Law, global justice and global empowerment' (Kaldor 2003a: 12).

Supporters of the Global Civil Society ideal have thus introduced a new notion of a global/transnational justice based on a transnational moral solidarity that links individuals, non-governmental organizations, social movements and global institutions. In this way, they link such a broader understanding of civil society to an idea of 'bottom-up' global justice.

Rather than a global representative democracy, this approach endorses a notion of global civil society as a 'functional equivalent' (Rosenau 1998) to democracy; 'global civil society cannot claim to "represent" the people in the way that formally elected states can and do.[...]NGOs have a voice not a vote. But the fact that global civil society is, in principle, voluntary and open to all individuals offers the possibility of participation and deliberation at global levels' (Kaldor 2003a: 141–42).

3.3
A NORMATIVE PROPOSAL FOR CIVIL SOCIETY

In the present book, a notion of civil society which encompasses the three streams studied before is suggested. A normative idea of civil society in contemporary multi-structured societies depends crucially on the coexistence of and the equilibrium among the three domains of culture economics and politics. In the previous sections, I have shown that in both Western political philosophy and contemporary usage civil society has been related to the realization of freedom either in the public or in the private realm. Furthermore, in both cases, it is possible to distinguish quite clearly three distinct versions of civil society with regard to these three domains.

In this section, I first recover Hegel's formulation of civil society. This analysis is meant to emphasize how political, economic and cultural features functioned in Hegel bourgeois society. Then, I link the idea of civil society to the idea of multiple identities. As I argued in the previous sections, civil society has been generally associated with the three spheres of culture, economy and politics.

In this work, the analysis of Hegelian bourgeois society plays a crucial role. Actually, any contemporary attempt to understand civil society cannot leave Hegelian work out of consideration. Although the analysis of pre-Hegelian formulations might be useful in order to reconstruct the developments of the idea of civil society, undoubtedly, only with Hegel did civil society assume a modern content becoming a crucial feature of modernity. Thus, the Hegelian framework is not only more likely to clarify the content of civil society, but it also represents a starting point for a modern understanding of this idea. In the present work, Hegel plays a fundamental role for a number of reasons:

- Civil society as distinct from state. Civil society appears as an intermediate sphere of the ethical life distinct from both family and state.
- Taking collective claims seriously. In this perspective, civil society is the product of a specific cultural and historical development; it is the realm where individuals are linked to each other by virtue of their plural affiliations.
- Civil society as the realm of individual freedom.

Finally, it is worth noticing that civil society, as proposed in the present work, has to be understood as a liberal reading of the Hegelian civil society. My aim is to save some Hegelian features that I take as necessary for conceiving of civil society as an intermediate dimension between 'family' and 'state'. In such a context, civil society is conceived not only as a bearer of specific historical developments, but also as bearer of universal values, such as individual freedom, human dignity necessary to preserve pluralism within society. Furthermore, the liberal account makes this framework individual-oriented rather than collective-oriented.

This use of civil society leads my proposal out of a liberal-universalistic understanding of politics. Apparently, the choice of Hegel could be useful for a descriptive analysis, because of its historical focus. However, the ideas of non-institutional agreement and culture of civility that derive from it are definitely normative.

3.3.1 From Hegel's bourgeois society to civil society

In the previous section, I have identified the domains of civil society. I have concluded that the issue of freedom implies three dimensions for civil society in the realms of culture, economy and politics. I argue here that Hegel's bourgeois society offers a synthesis of these competing views. This notion played a pivotal role in the development of the notion of civil society. Actually, many scholars tend to consider civil society as a modern post-Hegelian concept (Cohen and Arato 1994).

Hegel's formulation upheld and developed most of the FS stream's intuitions. Accordingly, civil society, as realm of particular interests, represented the starting point of his investigation.[14] However, it is true that, only with Hegel, would the typical contractarian antithesis, state of nature/civil society, have been overcome. In his framework, this antagonism was replaced by introducing a new, distinct but not necessarily opposed, couple of concepts: *bourgeois society* and state. Therefore, bourgeois society was the sphere of particular interests, representing an intermediate step between 'family' and 'state'. Rather than a kind of antistate, civil society assumed a specific character in the Hegelian dialectic: it was meant to generate universal principles in the ethical juridical sphere; so, it was supposed to characterize the content of the state itself.[15]

This formulation had significant implications on the modern notion of civil society. *Bourgeois society* was not the market, it was rather the realm of the capitalistic division of labour. Furthermore, it was supposed to be separated from the state, even comprising a public space, including a kind of politics, and a juridical system, and from family, even if it involved cultural and traditional features. While Aristotle had distinguished *polis* (πόλις) from oikos (οἶκος), where only the first was meant to represent the public domain, Hegel was suggesting three spheres: family, civil society and state.[16] Civil society was a pattern comprehensive of both public and private features, even though it was independent from both market and state. On this point, Taylor (1955: 222) has rightly argued that, in his concept of civil society, Hegel used independent associations for non-political purposes but

> [...] their significance is not that they form a non-political social sphere, but rather *that they form the basis for fragmentation and diversity within the political system*. [...] Thus, the different elements of Hegel's political society take up their role in the state [...]. In this way *we avoid both the undifferentiated homogeneity of the general will state, which Hegel thought must lead inevitably to tyranny and terror, and also the unregulated and ultimately self-destructive play of blind economic forces*, which then seemed to be menacing England. [Emphasis added]

In paragraph 182 of *Philosophy of Rights*, Hegel introduces his idea of civil society:

> [...] The concrete person, *who as particular is an end to himself, is a totality of wants and a mixture of necessity and caprice*. As such, he is one of the principles of the civic society. But the *particular person* is essentially connected with others. Hence, each establishes and satisfies himself by means of others, and so must call in the assistance of the form of universality. This *universality* is the other principle of the civil society. [Emphasis added]

Thus, Hegel recognized three institutions of ethical life: family, civil society and the state. His formulation of civil society included cultural, political and economic features in a peculiar way. It actually entailed three parts: the system of needs (*Bedürfnisse*), the administration of justice (*Rechtsflege*), the police (Polizei) and the corporation (*Korporation*).

Undoubtedly, the system of needs represented the economic side of Hegelian civil society:

> § 189: The particularity, which is in the first instance opposed to the universal will (§ 60), is subjective want. It gets objectivity, i.e., is satisfied (a), through external objects, which are at this stage the *property of others, and the product of their needs and wills, and (b) through active labour, as connecting link between subjective and objective*. Labour has as its aim to satisfy subjective particularity. Yet by the introduction of the needs and free choice of others universality is realized. Hence, rationality comes as an appearance into the sphere of the finite. This partial presence of ra-

tionality is the understanding, to which is assigned the function of reconciling the opposing elements of the finite sphere. [Emphasis added]

According to Rawls (2000: 344), the system of needs represented the 'economy' where individuals 'exchange goods and services to fulfil their needs and wants [...] [and] recognize that they are interdependent'. On this point, Hegel clarified:

> § 191: The satisfaction of want and the attainment of means thereto become a realized possibility for others, through whose wants and labour satisfaction is in turn conditioned. The abstraction, which becomes a quality of wants and means (§ 191), *helps to determine the mutual relation of individuals.* This general *recognition of others is the element which makes the isolated abstract wants and means concrete and social.* [Emphasis added]

Thus, the system of needs was clearly related to the FS stream. The bourgeois society was first of all the sphere where an individual's particularity emerged. Nevertheless, unlike the Scottish Enlightens, such a sphere includes the economic sphere but it is not limited to it. Actually, in addition to the 'system of needs' the Hegelian bourgeois society was meant to include a kind of juridical system (the *Rechtsflege*), and a third part, which entailed both cultural and political features. With reference to the third part, Hegel operated a distinction between two categories: police and corporation.

> Addition § 237: *Police control and provision are intended to intervene between the individual and the universal possibility of obtaining his wants.* It takes charge of *lighting the streets, building bridges, taxation of daily wants, even of health.* Two main views stand out at this point. One view is that it falls to the police to look after everything, the other that the police should not interfere at all, since everyone will be guided by the need of others. The individual, it is true, must have the right to earn his bread in this or the other way, but on the other hand the public has a right to ask that what is necessary shall be done [...]. [Emphasis added]

It would be misleading to believe that the Hegelian idea of *Polizei* can be understood in the light of the present idea of police. In truth, it implied something wider and more complex than that. In Hegel's scheme, *Polizei* was meant to derive its content from the Greek *politeia* (πολιτεία) (Rawls 2000: 345). It was much more than law enforcement and covered a wide range of activities that actually constituted the socio-political life of individuals in bourgeois society, '[...] it covered [...] also the fixing of the prices of necessities, the control of quality of goods, the arrangements of hospitals, street lighting, and much more' (ibid.). The administration of justice and the police had a main political function in civil society; they represented the political constrains that enabled self-interested individuals to overcome the 'system of needs' by creating a 'formal universality'.

Conversely, Hegel's corporation was supposed to function as further instance of particularity in a specific sense. In paragraph 255, Hegel introduced his idea of corporations:

> As the family was the first, so the corporation, grounded upon the civil society, constitutes the *second ethical root or basis of the state*. The family contains the elements of *subjective particularity and objective universality* in substantive unity. Then, in the civic community, these elements are in the first instance dissociated and become on the one side a particularity of want and satisfaction, which is turned back into itself, and on the other side abstract legal universality. The corporation joins these two in an internal way, so that particular wellbeing exists and is realized as a right. [Emphasis added]

By 'corporation' Hegel meant organizations of groups of workers, of religious and cultural associations, as well as town councils. It was neither a trade union nor a genuine political category; it rather covered the cultural side of the organization in civil society. Rather than denying the individualistic content of civil society, corporation represented an intermediate step between the 'competitive individualism' of the system of needs and the 'formal universality' of the administration of justice (Rawls 2000).

Hegel's corporation seemed to recover the content of Montesquieu's idea of 'intermediary bodies' (Montesquieu 1758). As the 'intermediary bodies', corporations were supposed to be a means of preserving a sense of place, of localness, of religion and identity (Mosher 1984). However, while Montesquieu's intermediary bodies were conceived in the framework of the state, corporation was an attribution of civil society. Thus, one can argue that the inclusion of those features (the judiciary, the police and corporation) made Hegel's idea of civil society so relevant, these elements actually distinguished his idea of civil society from those of other writers.

As Rawls (2000: 345) has pointed out,

> [...] civil society, as [Hegel] thought of it, was new to the modern state and characterized modernity itself. His view is distinctive in that he considers many aspects of what had been regarded as elements of the state,

as actually elements of civil society. See for example [...] the judiciary, the police and corporation. The political state is separate from civil society, while both together are the state in the wide sense'.

Thus, the idea of civil society, as proposed by Hegel, appeared as a 'complex equilibrium among conflicting forces and interests of the three domains of culture, politics, and economy'. In this way, Hegel created a stable form of reflective social and ethical life. Again, on this Rawls (ibid.: 346) argued, 'civil society and its institutions have an important role in making possible a stable form of reflective social life'. This stability depended crucially on the links among those three domains and the balance between particularity and universality. Actually, the tension among political, cultural and economic features played a key role not only in ensuring civil society as the realm of individual freedom, but also in making clear the separation between civil society and state.

Thus, in the light of this interpretation, Hegelian civil society overcomes the classical controversies between individual versus collective, or between public and private. In the bourgeois society, free individuals were embedded in a specific historical, cultural and social context. Coming back to the classical approaches to civil society, these suggest three different dimensions for civil society in the political realm. Taken in their extreme versions, one can synthesize three types of civil society:

Culturally oriented — it is the context in which individual freedom is sacrificed for the historical specific tradition of a given society.
Economically oriented — in such a case, civil society is a depoliticized and rational private sphere. Individual freedom is preserved in such an enlarged private sphere.
Politically oriented — it is the public sphere of the universal values; in this case there may emerge a clash between universal values and the recognition of the historical specific tradition of a given context.

Thus, each one of these cases can be understood as a degeneration of the normative model of civil society. In all these cases civil society, in fact, lacks that 'stable form of reflective ethical and social life' as it was conceived by Hegel. Thus, it is possible to argue that any approach that gives priority to one domain over the others is likely to deny the very idea of civil society. The paradoxical outcome of these models is that the emerging domain tends to overlap with the corresponding model of state. To use Hegel's words, the dialectic progression of the concepts of family, civil society, state is substituted only by two forms of ethical life: family and state.

3.4

CIVIL SOCIETY ENGAGEMENT IN DEEPLY DIVIDED SOCIETIES:
A THEORETICAL FRAMEWORK

The way in which scholars look at civil society's intervention in deeply divided societies varies with regard to their views about two relevant issues: their understanding of cultural identity in conflict, and their interpretation of civil society. Concerning the first problem, I have distinguished two main ways to interpret cultural identity in conflict: the primordialist-essentialist perspective and the constructivist-instrumental perspective. I have called primordialists those accounts that emphasize the collectivist nature of such conflicts where the 'groups' are supposed to be the main unit of analysis; while I have considered as constructivists those approaches that offer an individualistic perspective, which posits in individuals' rationality the responsibility to construct or manipulate sectarian identities and to fuel violence. Therefore, the primordialist approach entails a kind of cultural reductionism, while constructivism introduces a sort of individualist reductionism.

Recently, a vast literature focused on identity-based conflicts has emerged. However, between the extreme positions of those who support the idea of unavoidable 'ancient ethnic hatreds' (Huntington 1993, 1996; Ignatieff 1993, 1997; Kaplan 1993) and those who deny any significance of ethnic or cultural claims (Fukuyama 1992), three major approaches are extremely influential on on contemporary literature on the identity and conflict nexus: the Protracted Social Conflicts theory, the economic approach to 'greed versus grievances', and the political approach to 'new nationalism'.

The PSC theory, developed by Azar and Burton, imposes upon us to reconsider the levels of the analysis — generally based on the state level — focusing on the communal level. Multi-communal societies are characterized by the 'prolonged and often violent struggles among different communal groups for some "basic needs", such as security, recognition, and acceptance, fair access to political institution and economic participation' (Azar 1990: 93). This approach looks at the identity groups — i.e. ethnic, religious or racial groups — as the most useful unit of analysis and 'ethnic heterogeneity' is understood as 'structural precondition' for ethno-religious conflict (Gurr 2001, 2007).

Conversely, two further approaches present two versions of 'rational choice theory' applied to conflict. In the first case, in the economic approach to 'greed versus grievances', the emphasis is placed on some economic factors, such as low per capita income, slow economic growth and large exports of natural resources (Fearon 2005; Collier 2007). These features shape the basis of the conflict while rational actors use identity-based arguments to get popular support. In contrast to the PSC theory, such groups of actors are seen not as protest movements emerged in response to the needs deprivations of their community, but as 'the ultimate manifestation of organized crime' (Collier 2007: 198). Therefore, even though they would develop discourses on 'grievances', 'in practice' the identitarian motivation for these organizations is unimportant, what matters is 'whether the organization can sustain itself financially' (ibid.: 199): thus, the motivation for their violent actions is rooted in greed rather than grievance.

The second approach — 'new nationalism' — sees the emergence of new ideologies based on religious or ethnic features as the real source of conflict. These manufactured sectarian ideologies are aimed at legitimizing authoritarian leaders, new aspirants to power in moment of transition, or common criminals in their criminal actions (Brubaker and Laitin 1998, Brubaker 2004, Kaldor et al. 2007; 1999). Even though it shares the main idea of the economic approach, which assumes that greed rather than grievance motivates these actors, in this account, the role played by the 'new ideologies' becomes more relevant. According to this view, it would be misleading to believe that these ideologies — recently emerged in Eastern Europe as well as in several post-colonial countries — can be dismissed as unimportant. Actually, the emergence of such new forms of identitarian violence reflects deep political shifts linked to the phenomenon of globalization: societies have entered a new phase of insecurity that can be hardly framed within classical political categories, such as nation or territory. It would be therefore necessary to offer new political answers and categories able to face the current wave of identitarian violence (Kaldor 1999, 2003a and 2003b; Stubbs 1996).

With reference to civil society, it is possible to summarize at least three main positions. A first approach places civil society in the economic realm. A political account locates an independent civil society between both state and economy; in this context civil society is supposed to be a crucial means for performing shared political interests and for informing governments of citizens' fundamental needs. Finally, a third cultural-oriented account recognizes a kind of 'civility' in those sets of cultural traditions and historical heritage held by each society; it implies the possibility of having different versions of civil society with regard to different contexts.

The concept of civil society has been recovered only recently in the field of conflict transformation. All the earlier-mentioned approaches have in turn deeply influenced contemporary literature on conflict transformation; however, what seems to be relevant in such a context concerns the application of both reductionisms to the notion of civil society. On the one hand, scholars who look at identity-conflicts through the lenses of cultural reductionism tend to underline the 'collective' character of civil society. In such a perspective, civil society is understood as a fundamental stage of development in which different groups can recognize each other and cooperate. According to this perspective, if it is true that the communal level is the source of the identity-conflict, it is therefore necessary to work at this level in order to overcome the condition of conflict among the different ethnic or religious communities. On the other hand, supporters of the individualistic account of conflicts see civil society as the space where individual autonomy and shared political pursuits emerge. In this perspective, civil society represents such a 'middle ground' (Belloni 2001: 168) between individuals and the state; and it functions both as a constraint to state power and a means of realization of individuals' capacities. According to the individualistic account, a strong civil society is supposed to be a necessary condition for modern and viable democracies.

3.4.1 Cultural reductionism and cultural stream

Thus, following the culturalist perspective, civil society represents the intermediate ground where it is possible to mediate between a condition of pluralism, understood as different groups with their interests and goals, and the state. Rather than in antithesis to the governmental authority, civil society is understood as a sort of 'anticipation' of the more extensive experience of the state. It is a crucial stage in the development of people belonging to different communities, who have to deal with diversity. Therefore, before it is so at the state level, it is at the level of civil society that it is possible to mediate collective claims through the emergence of 'civic links' (Varshney 2003a: 43) across different communities.

The involvement of people belonging to different ethnic or religious groups in one cooperative system represents a way to create trust and a certain level of social solidarity and inclusiveness within society (ibid.). Accordingly, the emergence of new 'inter-communal civic links' are supposed to foster the reconciliation process among different ethno-religious groups, giving people the chance to recognize and include the 'others' in activities and shared experiences (Lederach 1997, 2001). Furthermore, the voluntary basis of the associational mechanisms of civil society improve people's living conditions reducing the economic marginalization and the inequalities within different groups, which constitute underlying causes of frustration and conflict (Charney 1999; Woolcock and Narayan 2000; Fisher 2006; Pickering 2006). In general, since its 'corporative' understanding of civil society, this first approach recognizes as civil society all those formal and informal institutions and organizations aimed at 'educating people for citizenship'.

3.4.2 Individualist reductionism and economic and political streams

Conversely, according to the second account, which considers civil society as the sphere of individuals' freedom in antithesis to that of the state, civil society is supposed to function as a key feature in supporting democratic transition, balancing individuals' aspirations and state authority. In this context, civil society is alleged to be the realm of toleration where the pluralistic integration of individuals is due to its participative and communicative mechanisms. These mechanisms provide the balance between private interests and governmental power insuring people freedom and offering them a wide set of opportunities for participation in social life.

In this context, supporters of the economic approach tend to give priority to an understanding of civil society as a 'counter-weight to state authority', stressing its constructive potential in addressing accountability and transparency in both political and economic sectors. Conversely, supporters of the political version of individualist reductionism see civil society as the sphere of civility and liberal values. According to them, a strong civil society that promotes non-sectarian identities — such as cosmopolitan groups, human rights groups or women groups — is needed for overcoming the nationalist ideologies that emerged during the conflict. It allows the process to move towards a common political culture based on peace and human rights values (Kaldor 2003a; Kaldor et al. 2007). Therefore, with reference to individual reductionism, a first group of scholars invokes civil society intervention to control state authority, while the second group tends to emphasize the independence of civil society from the state (see Table 3).

Table 3 - Different approaches to civil society in conflict transformation			
CULTURAL IDENTITY/ CONFLICT THEORIES/ CS APPROACHES	PSC THEORY	ECONOMIC APPROACH	'NEW NATIONALISMS' THEORIES
Cultural reductionism	Civil Society as 'anticipation' of the state: • facilitating the inter-ethnic dialogue, • endorsing reconciliation among different communities, • reducing economic inequalities among different groups		
Individualist Reductionism		Civil society as 'counterweight' to state authority • introducing a greater transparency in the resource sector (in particular in primary commodity) • promoting social and humanitarian services as alternative to the overbearing state	Civil society as a 'public sphere' of individual autonomy and liberal values • promoting non-sectarian identities • developing civility within society • information politics • accountability politics

3.5
CIVIL SOCIETY AND DEMOCRATIC TRANSITION:
THE IDEA OF 'CULTURE OF CIVILITY'

The idea of civil society presented in the previous pages entails a conception of civil society complex and historically rooted. If it is true that civil society represents a precise step in the development of the state, therefore an approach to conflict transition based on the idea of civil society is supposed to take into consideration all those associational mechanisms and market organizational modalities already existing within society.

This line of thought gives priority to a complex understanding of civil society that involves all those associational mechanisms existing between state and family. Thus, the alleged role of 'civil society', as a bearer of liberal and nonsectarian values, can work in practice only if those organizations are actually embedded in the social reality of the context of intervention. In the same way, the ability of those organizations to represent an actual counterweight to the state crucially depends on their actual capacity to represent the people. Thus, I suggest an approach to civil society primarily aimed at strengthening those forms of 'civility' already existing at the local level.

Therefore, the effectiveness of civil society involvement in post-conflict transition crucially depends on how much it actually represents the specificity of the country of intervention and the people living that country. However, although such an idea entails much of the Hegelian assumptions, it would be misleading to think that it denies any possibility for a synthesis between the specificity of historical traditions and the universality of values such as tolerance, and human dignity. As in Hegel's frame the individualistic assumption of the 'system of needs' mediates the sense of place, of localness, of religion and identity embodied by the idea of 'corporation'; here the balance among cultural, political and economic domains guarantees a mediation between individualism and cultural identifications and, therefore, between universalism of values and particularism of shared experiences and traditions.

The approach to conflict transition based on civil society has thus to take into consideration those aspects of 'civility' compatible with an autonomous democratic development of the country, especially with those universal values understood by people as necessary in order to overcome the boundaries that emerged during the conflict.

Several scholars are prone to believe that democratic institutions are necessary to sustain an inclusive and democratic civil society (Walzer 2003). Yet, as Walzer (ibid.: 79) argues 'the civility that makes democratic politics possible can

only be learned in the associational networks' which populate the sphere of civil society. In deeply divided societies, newly emerged institutional settlements are
the product of hard negotiations, which very often reflect the deep divisions that
emerged during the war. Citizens are generally excluded from these political processes and it would be hard to assume that they do recognize constitutional arrangements and institutions, as the result of an 'overlapping consensus'. However, members of divided societies are likely to express their voices and their opinions at the
level of civil society. The various associational mechanisms and modalities that
constitute civil society provide them with several formal and informal forums
through which they can articulate discourses and formulate judgements.

The various associational mechanisms does not manifest itself only through the level of the well-struc-
tured public sphere where public discussions are articulated, but also through the
level of private interests and deep convictions. Civil society can be therefore understood as that sphere which encompasses both public and private futures where
the linkages among individuals take form and are articulated through economic partnerships, voluntary associations and shared cultural and religious traditions.
At the level of civil society, individuals make the experience of pluralism and develop 'liberal dispositions' towards others (Rosenblum 2003: 107). Rosenblum
puts it in terms of 'psychology of moral development' and recovers Rawls's notion of the morality of associations (Rawls 1971) arguing that 'the experience of
pluralism cultivates the habit of differentiating among spheres and adjusting moral
conduct to them' (Rosenblum 2003: 114). Civil society is thus the sphere where
a form of decency might emerge, which is related to the development of a specific 'common form of life' cultivated at schools, in cultural associations, in voluntary associations and through economic linkages. In this sense, we might consider civil society as the sphere where a kind of 'consensus' over a common culture of civility takes form. Recovering Rawls's distinction between a public 'political culture' and 'background culture' (Rawls 2005), here the culture of civility is placed in between these two cultures; it is supposed to function as a ground
for mutual recognition.

The culture of civility represents a kind of non-institutional consensus on a
specific tradition of civility, made up of shared values and traditions, which enables individuals to articulate discussions and judgements which can be accepted by others. In this perspective, it might become a condition for addressing a
thin form of democratic deliberation in deeply divided societies. This culture is
not only concerned with political principles but also with religious beliefs and
non-public values: it can include both. This culture can range from a 'thin' kind
of procedural decency (making agreement in good faith, refusal of violence in public space), to the thickest forms of civility in which common substantive norms

(such as respect for differences, toleration, condemnation of racist rules) are accepted. Otherwise said, civil society needs to be understood as the sphere where individuals are able to recognize and deal with transitional issues by appealing to their common culture of civility.

Finally, it is necessary to clarify that 'civil society' cannot replace 'democracy'. In contemporary pluralistic societies, democracy requires an 'overlapping consensus' over a fundamental political conception. Furthermore, such a consensus is meant to include all the major democratic institutions, namely the basic structure of the society. Of course, the idea of a shared 'culture of civility' is not supposed to replace the moral consensus required for democracy. It is rather that 'dialogic part of the common human inheritance' (Sen 2006b) on which it is possible to build an autonomous path towards democracy.

What we need in post-conflict transition is to emphasize the common tradition of civility already existing in the society. Accordingly, the argument proposed in this work is that an effective approach to democratic transition has to start from below and has to take into account the cultural specificity and the common sense of justice emerging from those people who are actually involved in the democratization process. In those contexts, an ideal and universal value of democracy emerges as deeply linked to the preservation of human dignity and the restoration of pluralism through thin forms of public reasoning and tolerance.

NOTES

1. Definition of Civil Society adopted by London School of Economics, available on http://www.lse.ac.uk/collections/CCS/what_is_civil_society.htm (accessed in 2010).
2. At this level, the idea of civil society has to be understood as corresponding to political society.
3. With reference to the Greek notion of public space, it is useful to refer to Hannah Arendt. Although she can hardly be defined as a theorist of civil society, she emphasizes the relevance of the public space and of the specific kind of communicative power that this space generates. Her idea of public space has a clear connection with the ancient idea of *politeia*. See Arendt (1958).
4. With reference to this pre-Hegelian usage of civil society, 'Civil society is not a new post-Hegelian concept. It is a much older term, which entered into English usage via the Latin translation, societas civilis, of Aristotle's politicon koinonema. [...]' (Kaviraj and Khilani 2001: 17).
5. 'The right of nature, which writers commonly call jus naturale, is the liberty each man hath to use his own power as he will himself for the preservation of his own nature; that is to say, of his own life; and consequently, of doing anything which, in his own judgement and reason, he shall conceive to be the aptest means thereunto' (Hobbes 1668, chapter XI).

6. It is interesting to notice here that Gramsci thought that from the point of view of cultural domination the Church is the typical example of civil society in history. See also Taylor (1995).
7. See chapter II, § 6, 8, 9 (Locke 1824).
8. Chapter V.
9. With reference to this point, Smith's notion of 'invisible hand' played a crucial role. According to him, the disposition of things in society is seen as arising not out of any collective will or common decision, but by virtue of an 'invisible hand', a sort of providence (Ferguson 1767; Smith 1776).
10. For Locke, people in the state of nature lived under the subordination of God.
11. See also Putnam (1995); Cox (1999); Putnam and Pharr (2000); Chandhokhe (2005),
12. H. Arendt was the first to attack the concept of society as an intermediate realm between private and public. In her understanding, 'society' is definitely a public space. This achievement allows her to elaborate her theory of public space and the specific kind of communicative power that such space produces. However, Arendt considers the realm of social as inferior to that of politics (Arendt 1958).
13. See Locke (1824: chapter XVII, § 206, 207, 208).

14. With regard to this liberal understanding of Hegel's civil society see also Rawls (2000: 330): '[...] I interpret Hegel as a moderately progressive reform-minded liberal, [...]. I shall look at how Hegel thought the concept of freedom was actually realized in the political and social institutions at a particular historical moment.'

15. With reference to this, Bobbio (1976: 18) argued '[...] mentre lo Stato hobbesiano e rousseauiano esclude definitivamente lo Stato di natura, lo Stato hegeliano contiene la società civile [...]: la contiene e la supera trasformando una universalità meramente formale in una realtà organica, a differenza dello stato Lockeiano che contiene la società civile non per andare oltre ma per legittimarne l'esistenza e gli scopi' ('while for Hobbes and Rousseau the state is opposed to the state of nature, Hegel's state incorporates civil society: Hegelian state includes and overcomes civil society bringing the universality from a mere formality to an organic reality. Conversely, for Locke the state incorporates civil society to legitimize its scope[...]' (translation by the author).

16. About this point, Cohen and Arato (1994: xiv) have argued '[...] the Hegelian theory is crucial because it reconstructs civil society in terms of the three levels of legality, plurality and association, and publicity and because Hegel sees a link between civil society and state in terms of mediation and interpretation'.

And, from whatever time of day
and from whatever corner
you set your sights on Sarajevo,
you always and without specific intention
think the same thing.
That is a city.
A city that both nears its end and is dying,
yet simultaneously is being born and growing.

Ivo Andríc

Chapter 4

Civil society in Bosnia after Dayton:
a case study[1]

4.1 Understanding the Bosnian case: ethnic groups, nationalism in politics and international involvement – 4.2 Post-conflict transition and civil society building in Bosnia – 4.3 Bosnian culture of civility and transition to democracy – 4.4 The case of the Associations of Victims and Relatives of Missing Persons in Bosnia – 4.5 Concluding remarks

The war in Bosnia and Herzegovina (hereafter Bosnia) was the most deadly conflict in Europe since the Second World War. Today, more than 15 years after the end of the war, the path towards a viable and pluralistic democracy in Bosnia still seems difficult. Although, both scholars and practitioners alike from all around the world are increasingly paying attention to the democratic transition in the region, the country still presents signals of deep instability at both economic and political levels. The political system shows the traits of a 'hybrid regime' (Bojkov 2003: 42) where democratic institutions coexist with un-democratic mechanisms. In this system, both forces are necessary in order to sustain a certain level of stability in the country (ibid.). In addition, despite international efforts, an actual dialogue among the three former warring parties is still far from being fully achieved. The ethnic division of the population represents a major challenge to both territorial integrity and political unity, while nationalist parties are maintaining a predominant role in the political realm. Recently, much scholarly work has been done on the constructive potential of civil society engagement in post-conflict contexts. Civil society intervention is supposed to foster democracy from the bottom shaping those universal values needed to 'civilize' deeply divided societies (Belloni 2001). Furthermore, it is considered to be a crucial transitional factor since it is seen as the sphere where it is possible to pacify societies by handling all conflicts non-violently and democratically (Orjuela 2003). Such positive expectations for civil society engagement played a fundamental role in the case of Bosnia; especially when, at the end of the 1990s, the failure of the approach based on the idea of international governance, as it was designed in the Dayton Agreements, emerged. In this context, engaging civil society actors in the transitional process was supposed to promote more substantive levels of democratic stability, combined with a higher degree of tolerance and pluralistic integration within society. In the light of this, in recent years there has been an extensive effort to build civil society in the country.

Nevertheless, the idea of 'civil society building', largely supported by international scholars and practitioners, has presented ambivalences and disintegrative potentials in its application to Bosnian reality (Belloni 2001). Because of the external financial and political dependence of most of the civil society actors operating in Bosnia, its actual impact has been mostly unproductive of those results invoked by international community. Additionally, such efforts have largely ignored all those associational mechanisms, participation modalities and market structures, which represent an important side of civil society (Pouligny 2005). The idea of 'civil society building' has constantly obstructed the inclusion of local forms of civil society in a constructive dialogue with governmental institutions. This has contributed to the creation of the model of 'governance without participation' (Bieber 2002: 26) which has characterized recent Bosnian political developments. Further, this approach to civil society has significantly reduced the possibility for Bosnian people to develop, at a private level before a public one, a common sense of civility necessary to achieve a sustainable democratic transition. Actually, the lack of participation has led Bosnian citizens to perceive such efforts as an external attempt to impose ideals and values inapplicable to the Bosnian context. Thus, they have increasingly looked at nationalist parties and movements as a genuine expression of Bosnian reality in contrast to the 'externality' of non-governmental actors (Belloni 2001).

This chapter criticizes current practices of 'civil society building' drawing on the results of a recent case study I conducted, which is focused on a peculiar kind of Bosnian civil society actors, the associations of victims and relatives of missing persons. It is based on interviews with representatives of these associations that were carried out during a field trip in Sarajevo in December 2007. It is structured as follows: the first section offers an introduction to the major challenges to democratic transition in the country. The second is devoted to a description of the current practices of 'civil society building'. The third chapter introduces an alternative conception of civil society more complex and historically rooted. Finally, the last section is focused on the case study. Here, the materials from literature and field work are used in an integrated way. The study aims to show that the approach based on the idea of common 'culture of civility' is more likely to emphasize the constructive potential of these actors in Bosnian democratic transition.

4.1
UNDERSTANDING THE BOSNIAN CASE: ETHNIC GROUPS,
NATIONALISM IN POLITICS AND INTERNATIONAL INVOLVEMENT

The lack of a durable reconciliation among the three major ethno-religious forces still constitutes the main obstacle to the democratic development of Bosnia. Four major issues are deeply challenging the peaceful coexistence of the three ethnic groups.

(1) The first problem concerns the territorial division of the country into two ethnic entities, the Serb RS and the Croat-Bosniak FBiH.[2] The recognition of the two entities was supposed to offer a solution to the ethnic division of the country, without affecting the territorial unity of the emerging state of Bosnia. However, the decision to recognize a relative autonomy to the two ethnic entities is likely to frustrate the expectations of both, the Serb and Croat-Bosniak sides. Actually, on the one hand the Bosnian Serbs have always looked at the notion of 'entity' as the outcome of the international community's intention to deny their right to self-determination, narrowing their status of 'people' to that of 'minority group'. On the Croat-Bosniak side, instead, the institution of the two entities has been perceived as the most important challenge to the territorial integrity. In sum, the institution of the two entities has represented a hybrid territorial compromise between an approach to conflict transition aimed at bringing together ethnic differences, based on the ideas of territorial autonomy and power-sharing (Lijphart 1991, 2004), and a more traditional approach directed to put emphasis on the relevance of the territorial integrity of the newly emerged state.

(2) The role of nationalist parties in the political life of contemporary Bosnia constitutes the second fundamental challenge to the country's democratic transition. The importance of nationalist actors has increased in the last years, this phenomenon being both cause and effect of the ethnic tensions in the territory. The power of nationalist parties in the political arena translated not only into a general ethno-religious approach to politics, but also into a kind of 'institutionalization of ethnicity' in the country through the introduction of settlements and mechanisms directed at the protection of a special representation of the three major ethno-religious groups (Bieber 2004). Although the Bosnian political realm suffers from the lack of actual alternatives to ethnic forces, it is relevant to note that the nationalist parties' leadership is recognized by a vast part of Bosnian population, especially in the rural areas.

(3) The revival of nationalist forces cannot be understood without taking into account the strategy of 'interventionism' adopted by the international community in the country (Belloni 2001; Pouligny 2005). Although the intention of in-

ternational actors was to weaken the influence of nationalist parties in Bosnian politics, this practice of intervention had the undesired effect of relieving nationalist leaders of the responsibility for their political actions, and increasing people's detachment from political life. International community interventionism has not only undermined the endogenous political and economic development of the country, but also contributed to emphasizing the link between people and nationalist forces.

(4) The lack of an integrate reform of the civil and criminal justice system suggests the last feature of instability. In spite of the efforts towards reforming the police system, the path towards a substantial reorganization of the system of justice is still far from being achieved.[3] Again, the major effects of this deficit of justice fall on the ethno-religious divisions in a dramatic way. In this context, the main obstacle concerns the reluctance on the part of both entities to cooperate with each other to create an integrated and accountable system of justice. Accordingly, representatives of both sides have increasingly boycotted any development in this sense. The effects of this are evident especially with respect to criminal justice: notwithstanding the international efforts, representatives of both entities have constantly obstructed any action of the International Criminal Tribunal for former Yugoslavia (hereafter ICTY), not only by refusing to collaborate with the international institution, but also by hiding and protecting most of the people charged with war criminal actions (Amnesty International 2003). The fact that most of the war criminals are still at large deeply questions the possibility of overcoming the divisions imposed by the conflict and developing a path of reconciliation among the three ethno-religious groups.[4]

4.2
POST-CONFLICT TRANSITION AND CIVIL SOCIETY BUILDING IN BOSNIA

In recent years, 'strengthening civil society' has been an imperative vastly invoked by the international community with reference to post-conflict societies (Paffenholz and Spurk 2006; Orjuela 2003; Lederach 2001; Varshney 2001). In Bosnia, civil society structures and mechanisms have functioned as both a means to mediate between international community and the three ethnic groups and tools to experience a bottom-up approach to democracy in the region (Fisher 2006). Although the Dayton Agreement largely ignored the issue of civil society (ibid.) the international community has strongly encouraged and supported civil society engagement so as it has become a main focus of the international involvement (Belloni 2001). In the last years, this country has experienced what is considered the most ambitious experiment in civil society engagement in a transitional society (Fisher 2006).

Scholars and practitioners have increasingly looked at the Bosnian conflict as the prototype of 'new conflict' (Kaldor 1999), where constructed sectarian ideologies functioned for supporting interests and actions of those leaders, mostly criminals, who wanted to gain power (Kaldor 1999; Kalyvas and Sambanis 2005). In this perspective, the emergence of a strong civil society sector is seen as a means to contrast the power of ethnic leaders by stimulating new socio-economic links and facilitating the emergence of trust, transparency and accountability. In particular, local and international grass roots NGOs are seen as key actors in fostering non-sectarian ideologies based on liberal and pluralistic values as an actual alternative to nationalist power (Kaldor 2003a; Kaldor et al. 2007).

However, Bosnian experience has shown the ambivalences raised by such an approach to civil society. The efforts to impose a model of civil society that is the bearer of 'Western civility' have constantly clashed with local values and traditions (Belloni 2001). Such a 'top-down' imposition of an external model of 'civility' has led Bosnian citizens to refuse it. Therefore, while the international community was prioritizing the process of 'civil society building' understood as an indispensable feature for the long-term stability of the region, increasingly Bosnians were not recognizing this 'external' civil society as an actual expression of their interests and needs. Most of them perceived this external imposition as an attempt to deny their own tradition of 'civility', rooted in a long history of tolerance and pluralism (Donia and Fine 1994, Belloni 2001). Because of this, in the last few years, nationalist forces have progressively regained popular support. The failure of international actors in building a crucial space of civic participation and freedom has led Bosnians to look at nationalist parties as the sole alternative to international interventionism.

Besides the psychological impact on Bosnian citizens due to its 'externality', there is also a theoretical problem connected to the very content of the idea of civil society. The Western-oriented approach to 'civil society building', as it has been applied to Bosnia, has seemed to neglect the historical variety of representations of the local social reality, which have always been linked to the notion of civil society (Pouligny 2005). Actually, the very idea of 'civil society building' clashes with an understanding of civil society that takes into account specific traditions of civic engagement, market actors and local mechanisms of participation. In Bosnia, the practice of 'civil society building' has excluded local organizational modalities, giving priority to the non-governmental sector — grass root NGOs. In this context, the non-governmental sector has functioned as a 'technical task', a feature for 'allocating financial resources and delivering services', rather than a means to overcome ethnic fragmentation (Belloni 2001: 163).

In contrast with the current practices, I wish to drawn on an idea of civil society more complex and historically rooted, which is aimed at emphasizing the specific culture of civility as a basis for an autonomous democratic development of Bosnian society.

4.3

BOSNIAN CULTURE OF CIVILITY AND TRANSITION TO DEMOCRACY

In their *Civil Society and Political Theory* Cohen and Arato have noted that any contemporary attempt to understand civil society cannot leave Hegel out of consideration (Cohen and Arato 1994). In his *Philosophy of Right*, the German scholar introduced a couple of new, distinct but not necessarily opposed, concepts: bourgeois society and state (Hegel 1966). Bourgeois society was the sphere of particular interests placed between 'family' and 'state'. It assumed a specific character in the Hegelian dialectic: it was meant to generate universal principles in the ethical juridical sphere; it was supposed to characterize the content of the state itself. This formulation had significant implications on the modern notion of civil society. According to Cohen and Arato (1994: xiv),

> [...] the Hegelian theory is crucial because it reconstructs civil society in terms of the three levels of legality, plurality and association, and publicity and because Hegel sees the link between civil society and state in terms of mediation and interpenetration.

According to Hegel, civil society was a pattern comprehensive of both public and private features, even though it was independent from both market and state. On this point, as I already noted in the previous chapter, Taylor argued that, in his concept of civil society, Hegel used independent associations for non-political purposes, but

> [...] their significance *is not that they form a non-political social sphere, but rather that they form the basis for fragmentation and diversity within the political system.* [...] Thus, the different elements of Hegel's political society take up their role in the state, [...]. In this way we avoid both the undifferentiated homogeneity of the general will state, which Hegel thought must lead inevitably to tyranny and terror, and also the unregulated and ultimately self-destructive play of blind economic forces, which then seemed to be menacing England. (Taylor 1995: 222). [Emphasis added]

According to this perspective, civil society represents a counter-weight to the 'tyranny of the state' but it also corresponds to a kind of 'anticipation' of the more extensive experience of the state. Therefore, if it is true that civil society represents a particular step in the development of the state, therefore an approach to conflict transition based on the idea of civil society should take into consideration all those local modalities which are generally excluded by the current practices of civil society building. This sensibly reduces the relevance of grass root NGOs. The alleged role of these actors, as bearers of liberal and non-sectarian values, can work in practice only if these organizations are really embedded in the local social reality. Similarly, the ability of these organizations to represent an actual counterweight to the state power crucially depends on their actual capacity to represent the citizens. Thus, in contrast with the idea of 'civil society building', the present chapter entails an approach to civil society primarily aimed at strengthening those forms of civility already existing at the local level.

However, it would be misleading to think that the proposed approach denies any possibility for a synthesis between the specificity of historical traditions and the universality of values such as tolerance, pluralism and freedom. In Hegel's framework, the individualistic assumption of the 'system of needs' mediates the sense of place, of localness, of religion and identity embodied by the idea of 'corporation' (Rawls 2000: 345). This produces a mediation or, to put it in Hegel's words, a 'synthesis' between universalism of values and relativism of cultural traditions. In this perspective, civil society can be understood as the sphere where a common 'culture of civility' emerges. Here, the 'culture of civility' is supposed to function as grounds for mutual recognition. The 'culture of civility' can be understood as a kind of preinstitutional 'consensus' on a specific tradition of civility, made up of shared values and traditions, which enables people to become part of a moral community. This culture is not only concerned with political principles, neither only with religious beliefs or non-public values, but it can include both. In this perspective, it can range from a 'thin' kind of 'procedural decency' (making agreement in good faith, refusal of violence in public space), to the thickest forms of civility in which common substantive norms (as respect for differences, toleration, condemnation of authoritarian rules) are accepted.

In the case of Bosnia, it is possible to recognize at least two of those features of 'civility'. Bosnian history of the last century has been marked by two dramatic experiences: the militarization of Tito's regime and the identitarian violence fuelled by ethno-politics. However, a reaction to both militarism and ethnic hatreds comes up from the history of Bosnian society, which is part of what I call 'Bosnian tradition of civility'. This tradition has been articulated in two specific ways. First, the actual usage of the term civil society in Bosnian language has to be understood as something different from the military sphere. Rather than participation or any other classical meaning, in its traditional usage *civilno druvsto* was referred 'to something not from the military' (Large 1997: 112). In the face of the depersonalized military structures, the idea of civility, as understood by Bosnians, is supposed to reform the human relationships in opposition to those forms of despotic interference operated by the authoritarian regimes (ibid.: 113).

A second feature of 'civility' is linked to a peculiar form of pluralism and tolerance inherited from the Ottoman Empire and its Millet system. Bosnian civil society has always been characterized by a kind of 'institutionalized communitarianism' (Bougarel 1996). As Donia and Fine have shown, Bosnians share a common culture which is the product of ages of common history. Bosnia has been a coherent entity for centuries, and it 'has shown over these centuries that pluralism can successfully exist even in a Balkan context' (Donia and Fine 1994: 9). In this context, the idea of *komšiluk* still expresses a notion of friendly relation 'based on respect and reciprocity between people belonging to different communities' (Belloni 2001: 169).

4.4
THE CASE OF THE ASSOCIATIONS OF VICTIMS AND RELATIVES
OF MISSING PERSONS IN BOSNIA[5]

The foregoing discussion suggests that it is necessary to understand the relationship between civil society and 'culture of civility' and how we should study local associational modalities in the light of it. The present case study is aimed at offering a first research hypothesis in this sense. To this end, this section offers an analysis of a specific group of actors which strongly represents Bosnian social reality: the Associations of Victims and Relatives of Missing Persons (hereafter AVRMP). With respect to these associations, I first discuss the problems raised by the application of the approach to 'civil society building'. I subsequently offer some arguments to prove that an approach more sensitive to the Bosnian tradition of civility is more likely to be effective. Finally, I describe the role played by these actors in the democratic transition of the country.

The AVRMP are non-profit organizations, made up mostly of women — wives or mothers of victims and missing persons — which emerged in Bosnia soon after the last war. Most of them present an intra-ethnic composition. Initially, their aim was to find missing persons and recover their bodies for proper burial. Today, as a result of their increased relevance in the socio-political realm, these associations are articulating more ambitious goals. They are engaged in a political struggle for the public recognition of the human dignity of the victims and the condemnation of war crimes. Therefore, these actors represent the complexity of the contemporary Bosnian socio-political realm: on the one hand, they are linked to the respective nationalist parties; on the other hand, they are aware of the necessity to cooperate with each other to overcome the atrocities of the war. In particular, some of these associations play a fundamental role in addressing common political issues, such as the reform of the judicial system and the arrest of all war criminals still at large.

With reference to the AVRMP, one might first show the limits of the most popular approach based on the idea of 'civil society building'. As already noted, this approach has led international scholars and practitioners to pay growing attention to those grass roots NGOs that promote non-sectarian identities focusing on liberal universal values, such as human rights or women rights. In particular, the idea of 'civil society building' in Bosnia has been associated with the alleged mission of the NGOs to 'civilize civil society' (Belloni 2001). In the case of the AVRMP, supporters of 'civil society building' approach might follow two distinct strategies.

One strategy would be to simply ignore these associations. According to this perspective, the AVRMP represent locally based interests and, what is even more important, present ambivalences and disintegrative potentials when they are associated with nationalist parties. The second strategy, instead, might be more likely to take into consideration these actors emphasizing their non-sectarian practices. For instance, it might lead to labeling such groups as bearers of women rights because of their predominantly female composition. In line with the experiences of other groups of women in other regional contexts (Kaldor 2003a; Kaldor et al. 2007; Keck and Sikkink 1998) supporters of this view are prone to consider collaboration and interaction of these associations with grass root NGOs and international institutions as a positive way of emphasizing non-sectarian values, such as women rights, in order to divert the attention from sectarian ideologies. Both approaches have major flaws: not only do they fail to understand the actual impact of the AVRMP in the Bosnian socio-political realm but they also override the real content of such actors' claims.

The first strategy, that simply ignoring these associations gives them no alternative to nationalist parties, while the second strategy raises two main problems. First, in spite of the predominantly female composition, it would be misleading to believe that these associations are prone to foster women rights. In Bosnian society, feminism as an ideology is still deeply weak and, in general, the role of women in the socio-political realm is still perceived as regrettable (Helms 2007). The category of 'woman' at the public level is generally allowed only when it is associated to the 'victimization' of the period of the war. This explains why in the last years several associations of mothers, widows, and victims of wartime rapes have emerged in Bosnia: they represent the archetype of this form of 'victimization'. Most of these women emphasize 'the apolitical and therefore noble character of their work' (ibid.: 241). An approach focused on universal values is an ineffective one, since it entails Western categories — in this case feminist values — which do not necessarily reflect Bosnian women's claims. The second argument can be seen as a consequence of the ineffectiveness discussed before. In this sense, the approach to 'civil society building' is likely to create a vicious circle: due to their externality, grass roots NGOs and international organizations cannot establish a durable cooperation with these associations and, consequently, these actors find in the respective nationalist parties more collaborative and stable partners.[6]

Conversely, the approach based on the idea of 'culture of civility' overcomes the limitations of the other approach, since it is rooted in the Bosnian tradition. It is aimed at facing the challenges of the ethno-politics, as it gives these women the chance to be involved in the democratic development of the country. In this perspective, the ambivalent attitude of these women with respect to their links to nationalist parties can be explained as a form of reaction to the international community efforts to impose on them an external notion of 'civility'. The issue of the links with their respective nationalist parties can therefore be challenged giving them a more detailed and satisfying substitute for nationalist politics.

Indeed, the specificity of Bosnian 'civility' is more likely to be understood by these women, since it entails traditions and values publicly recognized as a part of Bosnian culture. In this respect, it is worth noticing that many of the women interviewed were more likely to recognize themselves and their associations in terms of non-military and non-violent movements, in line with the tradition of non-militarism discussed before, than in terms of women groups.

> 'We were all victims of that dirty war.' '[...] There is no difference be-
> tween us [...]' '[...] we represent a non-military and peaceful response
> to that dirty war, our aim is to find the persons who are still missing [...]
> and give them public recognition.'[7]

Additionally, such an approach is prone to produce positive effects in terms of mutual recognition, due to its focus on shared values and traditions. During the interviews, several people appeared to recognize the necessity to foster a certain degree of inter-group dialogue and cooperation. Several women referred to the ancient tradition of the *komšiluk* and stressed the urgency to restart from the recognition of the existence of common values and traditions in Bosnian society, and the legacy of centuries of peaceful coexistence of the three religious groups:

> '[...] before the war we were friends, we all share the same traditions,
> in Visegrad, my village, ethnic hatred did not exist.'[8] '[...] We should
> appeal to the ancient Bosnian tradition of the *komšiluk*; we should co-
> operate as human beings, as mothers, as victims and as people belong-
> ing to different religious groups. Only when women from different as-
> sociations will understand the necessity to support each other, even be-
> longing to different religious groups [...], we will see in jail all war crim-
> inals and our quest of justice will be satisfied.[...]'[9]

4.4.1 Shared experiences and identities versus ethnic identity

The AVRMP strongly reflect post-war Bosnian social reality, since the emergence of these associations is both a reaction and a consequence of the ethnic conflict. Their members were among those people who paid the highest price for the war; yet, many of them currently reproduce the religious hatreds that emerged during the conflict, and are often closely linked to their respective nationalist parties. As I noted before, this is the most controversial aspect with reference to contemporary approaches to 'civil society building'. The linkage between these actors and nationalist leaders is either overemphasized by the supporters of the first strategy or underestimated by those of the second one. However, both approaches are prone to enhancing this link.

However, it is worth noting that all of the members of the AVRMP are aware of the similarity of their experiences as victims, as mothers and wives of missing persons. The relevance of shared experiences over the sense of belonging to a specific ethno-religious group is particularly evident for Mr Mehmed Musić, the president of the Association of Victims of Hadžići. Mehemed Musić, who was captured and tortured during the war, strongly defended his role of representative of all war victims in Hadžići, independent of their religious faith. According to Mr Musić, the condition of victims put all people on the same level, regardless of religious or ethnic belonging. For this reason, his association is based on an inter-ethnic communal/local solidarity. The idea of 'being a victim' associated with the strict localism of this association enables its members to overcome the ethnic boundaries that emerged during the war.[10]

The issue of the weight of ethno-religious affiliations seems to represent a major obstacle for other associations, in particular those directed by women. In contrast with the latter case, these associations often have a religious connotation, and sometimes the ethno-religious affiliation is required for membership. In addition, the predominantly female composition apart, their members strongly emphasize the rhetoric of victimhood extending it as far beyond sexual/gender matters to include their respective ethno-religious groups. Nevertheless, these women also recognize the relevance of their common experiences. In particular, most of them are likely to emphasize the common experience of 'mother-hood' associated with the tragic events of the war. They lost their children or saw them being captured, tortured and raped.

> One can be Serb, Muslim or Christian, from the urban areas or the rural ones, more or less educated, but we all share at least one thing, we are all mothers.[11]

Further, most of them are prone to recognize the necessity of inter-ethnic co-operation. In this respect, some of the interviewed women insisted on the opportunity to create a kind of umbrella association in order to facilitate communication and the exchange of information among the associations.[12] Therefore, the recognition of the 'motherhood' in public discourses and the actual collaboration among mothers of different associations represent a concrete improvement in the perspective of a common struggle for justice and truth.

4.4.2 Human dignity and quest of justice

What all these associations have in common is their struggle against the impunity of most of the war criminals. In contemporary Bosnia, the issue of impunity represents a main challenge for the democratic transition. Such a phenomenon is deeply questioning the process of the return of victims and displaced persons to their former homelands.[13] Today, the AVRMP are actively cooperating with national and international institutions (ICTY, International Commission for Missing Persons ICMP, Federal Commission for Missing Persons [FCMP], and Office for Tracing Detained and Missing Persons of Republic of Srpska [OTDMPRS]) and promoting national campaigns in favour of an inter-ethnic collaboration on these issues.

However, the idea of justice, as perceived by these actors, is different from that embodied by the ICTY. Most of the inter-viewed referred to an understanding of justice which implies a general attempt to recognize the intrinsic value of human dignity. On the one hand, it entails the refusal of violence as an attempt to forgive the atrocities of the conflict; on the other, it corresponds to a quest of recognition of the human dignity of all the victims of the war.[14] They distinguish a general pursuit of justice (*pravda*) from the idea of law (*pravo*) fostered by ICTY's lawyers (Delpla 2007). What is perceived by ICTY's lawyers and judges as a technical task, aimed at convicting criminals according to the 'principle of proportionality with the crime' (ibid.: 231) committed, is understood by these actors as an attempt to educate Bosnian people to a culture of peace that places at its core the respect of human dignity of all human beings.

In some interviews, people referred to the 'depersonalization adopted by lawyers and investigators working for the ICTY', which, according to them, would clash with their first purpose that is concerned with the recognition of the individual identity of the victims.[15] In this perspective, more relevant seems to be the work promoted by the ICMP, FCMP and OTDMPRS. These institutions, which are based in Bosnia, represent a kind of mediation between victims' claims and ICTY's judicial activities.[16]

The issue of the quest of justice can be understood as an expression of those general ideas of justice and democratic thinking which represent the content of the Bosnian 'culture of civility'.

4.5
CONCLUDING REMARKS

In this chapter, I outlined four major challenges to Bosnian democratic transition: 'institutional hybridism'; the 'institutionalization of ethnicity'; the condition of deep dependency of Bosnian politics and economy on the international community; and the deficit of justice in the process of reconciliation. In this context, the alleged constructive role of civil society crucially depends on its capacity to represent the sphere where individuals are able to recognize and deal with these problems by appealing to the Bosnian 'culture of civility'.

With reference to the case of the AVRMP, I have shown how this approach is likely to display the relevance of these actors in the Bosnian context. The common pursuit of justice and truth that holds together these associations in their struggle against impunity and for the recognition of the human dignity of all victims is weakening the links between them and their respective nationalist parties. Surprisingly, these actors are progressively articulating a common strategy in the direction of truth and justice. The judicial struggle against impunity is thus becoming a fundamental warning — 'never again' — to Bosnian citizens. New affiliations and shared experiences, such as 'motherhood' or 'being victim', are becoming meaningful in this struggle. In this sense, the constructive potential of these associations for Bosnian democratic transition is threefold. First, they are addressing a crucial issue for Bosnian democracy, which is linked to a substantial reform of the judicial system aimed at emphasizing the value of human dignity of all human beings. Second, the common struggle for justice is displaying new possibilities for the actual cooperation among human beings who, even belonging to different religious groups, share a common tradition of 'civility'. Third, through their efforts in addressing values, such as human dignity and justice, they are translating these issues from the private level of their own experiences to the public level of the experience of all those potentially and actually threatened and victimized by the inhumanity of ethnic violence.

NOTES

1. The present case study has been already published in Marchetti and Tocci (2011).
2. The FBiH is further split into 10 ethnic cantons.
3. On 11 April 2008, after years of disputes, the lower house of the Parliament of Bosnia finally approved the final document of the police reform, which aims at integrating the country's two police forces. For more information, see http://news.bbc.co.uk/1/hi/world/europe/7341857.stm (accessed 14 January 2013).
4. However, the last few years have seen the capture of Radovan Karadic, former Bosnian Serb leader, indicted for genocide and crimes against humanity committed from 1992 to 1995 in Bosnia, on 21 July 2008 and Ratko Mladic, commander of the Serbo Army of Republic Srpska, widely recognized as responsible for the siege of Sarajevo (1992–95) and the Srebrenica massacre (1995), on 26 May 2011.
5. This section is based on qualitative research carried out during a field trip in Bosnia in December 2007. The interviews were based in Sarajevo. Due to my poor knowledge of Bosnian, most of those were carried out with the support of an interpreter. For this case study, a number of associations of relatives and local and international institutions cooperating with them have been selected. I was in contact with the following associations: Association of Citizens Srebrenica Mothers based in Srebrenica; Association of Families of Missing Persons of Sarajevo based in the Romanija region in Eastern Sarajevo; Board of Families of Captured Soldiers and Missing Civilians, Istocno Sarajevo based in Eastern Sarajevo; Association of Citizens Women of Podrinje based in Ilidža; Association of families of missing persons Visegrad 92 based in Sarajevo; Association for tracing captured and missing from Hadzici based in Hadzici; Association of Mothers of Srebrenica and Zepa Enclaves based in Sarajevo; Association of families of missing persons of Municipality Vogosca based in Vogosca; Association of Citizens Women of Srebrenica based in Tuzla; ICMP; FCMP.
6. Many of the women interviewed declared that they did not share their scopes and objectives with most of the INGOs and the international organizations that are based in Bosnia.
7. Hedija Kasapović, Association Visegrad 92, interview on Saturday, 1 December 2007; Milan Mandić, Association of Sarajevo-Romanija region interview of Saturday, 1 December 2007; Munira Subasić, Association of Srebrenica and Zepa enclaves, interview of Monday, 3 December 2007.

8. Hedija Kasapović, Association Visegrad 92, interview of Saturday, 1 December 2007.
9. Miriana Simanić, Association of Istocno Sarajevo, interview of Sunday, 2 December 2007.
10. Mehmed Musić, Association of Victims of Hadžići, interview of Friday, 30 November 2007.
11. Hedija Kasapović, Association Visegrad 92, interview of Saturday, 1 December 2007, Ema Čekić, Association of Municipality Vogosca, interview of Sunday, 2 December. Munira Subašić, Association of Srebrenica and Zepa enclaves, interview of Monday, 3 December 2007.
12. Miriana Simanić, Association of Istocno Sarajevo, interview of Sunday, 2 December 2007.
13. In some cases, people declared they were still victims of the threats of people who attacked them during the war. Ajiša Bektić, one of the few women who returned to Srebrenica, denounced the fact that most of the people who carried out the ethnic cleansing in the city were still living there and increasingly threatening the few Muslim people who had returned to their houses after the war. Ajiša Bektić, Association of Mothers of Srebrenica, interview of Monday, 3 December 2007.
14. As rightly pointed out by Delpla (2007: 218), in this context '[…] justice is not an intermediate category between vengeance and forgiveness; rather it is placed in opposition to vengeance and can also include forgiveness'.
15. Munira Subašić, Association of Srebrenica and Zepa enclaves, interview of Monday, 3 December 2007.
16. In particular, the ICMP is strongly collaborating with victims' associations by providing means and structures for the exhumation and recognition of bodies; in recent years it has also launched a huge DNA identification programme based in Sarajevo and Tuzla.

Conclusion

Since the end of the Cold War, ethno-religious conflicts have been the main cause of humanitarian catastrophes and a major threat to both local and international peace and stability. As a consequence of these tensions, deep divisions along ethnic and religious lines have increasingly emerged in several regions of the world. After years of ethnic violence and atrocities, in societies like Bosnia or Rwanda people do not recognize themselves as members of a political community, and identity politics is pursued, often in violent forms, at the expense of liberal democratic projects and reconciliation programmes.

The present book has explored the nature and role of civil society in deeply divided societies. Civil society has been presented here as the sphere where a shared 'culture of civility' emerges. The 'culture of civility' enables individuals to become part of a community of citizens and accept to reciprocate on the basis of some basic universal values, such as the protection of human dignity. The last chapter on Bosnia has shown that the relevance of civil society crucially depends on its capacity to represent the sphere where individuals are able to recognize and deal with transitional issues by appealing to the Bosnian 'culture of civility' and developing a sense of justice based on a shared understanding of the idea of human dignity.

In conclusion it is necessary to refer to the problem of the 'bad society' and clarify how the idea of culture of civility responds to it. In this respect, several scholars have warned that the focus on civil society is risky since it might include actors who play a key role in perpetuating ethnic polarization and violence, or what is called 'bad civil society' (Belloni 2008; Chambers and Kopstein 2001). In this view, domestic civil society often reflects the same form of segmentation that characterizes the political structure of divided societies. Thus, if, on the one hand, the inclusion of civil society in the transitional processes improves its legitimacy, on the other, it 'may come at the cost of efficiency by increasing the number of actors involved and thus making the decision-making process more burdensome' (Belloni 2008: 183). However, as Dryzek (2005: 231–32) rightly points out 'calling the state to the rescue of bad civil society is problematic if the state itself is the instrument of one group in a divided society, or if it is engaged in a homogenization project to bolster its own support'. State institutions can only partially represent the solution to the deep divisions that emerge in these societies. In addition, if civil society is as polarized as political society, it is crucial to find a ground for reconciliation in this sphere to make reconciliation at least conceivable at the state level.

Nevertheless, it is necessary to clarify here that the idea of culture of civility does not disregard the existence of deep divisions within these societies, neither does it assume that a climate of trust and tolerance has always existed before the ethnic or religious tensions. With reference to the first point, very often civil society is as polarized as political society. It becomes therefore extremely difficult to distinguish between a segment of civil society which actually fosters civic values from those actors which reflect the same forms of division that characterize the state, and, in many cases, the groups of victims and prosecutors reflect this polarization. However, the forms of decency linked to the idea of the culture of civility can only be learnt through the inclusion of all the actors — even those responsible for violations — in deliberative processes.

Second, although it would be misleading to assume that forms of peaceful coexistence have always existed in all these societies, it is worth noting that ethnicity or religion cannot be considered per se as divisive factors. In general, the thesis of the alleged incendiary effect of religion on politics cannot grasp the complexity of the relationship between citizens' comprehensive doctrines and public political culture in contemporary liberal democracies, and it is not sufficiently supported by empirical evidence (Eberle 2002; McGraw 2010). In particular, as we have seen in the previous pages, in most divided societies ethnic or religious divisions are the product of years of war and ethnic violence nurtured by the condition of capability-deprivation and lack of recognition within society. As I have discussed in the previous chapters, several empirical studies have shown that ethnic and religious heterogeneity does not represent per se an obstacle to peace, democracy and stability. In many divided societies some economic factors, political interests rather than ethnic or religious divisions are at the root of the conflicts. These features shape the basis of the conflict while identity-based arguments become a strong instrument of consent. In this perspective, the idea of culture of civility becomes necessary to break the vicious circle of ethnic and religious violence and can contribute to put forth the moral basis for the creation of new forms of citizenship by challenging the culture of impunity and reaffirming the human dignity of all individuals.

Post-scriptum

On the idea of culture of civility: some thoughts

by Neera Chandhoke

By the 1970s, intellectuals in Eastern/Central Europe had realized that the two options that had been historically available for radical politics, were simply not for them. The first option was reform of state power from above. The second was that of revolution from below. Both these paths had been ruled out by the Brezhnev doctrine; that the erstwhile Soviet Union would not hesitate to intervene if any attempt was made to destabilize the socialist world. The consequences were somewhat momentous, for if the doctrine reinforced the power of arbitrary bureaucracies and political elites in actually existing socialist societies, it also provoked deep reflection on the sort of strategies that could be profitably employed to beat an authoritarian system.

One such novel idea was that citizens should turn their collective backs on Stalinist states, and carve out a 'free zone' in society. This zone, which rapidly came to be populated by social associations, self-help clubs, and solidarity networks, the East Europeans called 'civil society'. Civil society was expected to be self-limiting insofar as it had no intent of taking over state power; it was democratic in opposition to political parties and trade unions, and it was anti-bureaucratic because it shunned organization and preferred loose decentred networks of social associations.

In a relatively short period of time, however, these self-limiting associations developed into a powerful political movement against arbitrary bureaucracies. The upsurge was spontaneous, unorganized, and haphazard, but it bore results. In 1989 some ostensibly powerful states collapsed like the proverbial house of cards before agitating and agitated crowds assembled in the streets. Political commentators in the west hastened to proclaim an end to an ideology and to a world: '*1989; Annus Mirabilis* — Year of Wonders'. And the political commentator Timothy Garton Ash wrote the obituary of socialism with some delight: 'This was the year Communism in Eastern Europe Died. R.I.P. 1949–1989.' The end of actually existing socialist societies, it was unanimously accepted, had been enabled by civil society.

Somewhat naturally the concept of civil society came onto the lips of political agents and policy makers as an antidote to everything that is undesirable in politics, from non-performing states to dictatorial regimes. If multilateral agencies and donors prescribed the building of civil society in authoritarian states as the one route to democracy, civil society in many other circles was expected to perform tasks till then supposed to fall within the provenance of the state, such as education, nutrition, and everything else that went under the rubric of development. But there is more, for political theorists are of the opinion that civil society can be entrusted with other responsibilities as well. In this politically significant work, Valentina Gentile allots to civil society the brief of creating, sustaining and reproducing a culture of civility in a post-conflict society, with a focus on that of Bosnia.

The wider question she addresses is the following: how do societies that have experienced intense ethno-nationalist hatred, which have split along the lines of polarized identities, where members have turned on each other in murderous fashion, and where once a collective 'we' has fragmented into a multiplicity of 'I' versus 'you', recreate a particular project; that of 'living together'. Gentile does not underestimate the enormity of the effort required to construct a culture of civility. Nor does she underrate the difficulties in recreating civil society in contexts where the pre-conditions of this space have simply gone missing amidst fratricidal ethnic conflict and blood lust.

For civil society cannot be taken for granted, it requires certain preconditions, such as mixed neighborhoods, participation in political movements across identity and class, and shared associational life. When social networks have been rent asunder by ethnic conflict, the restoration of what Gentile calls a 'culture of civility' based on the values of mutual respect and toleration is a project fraught with insurmountable difficulties. Gentile sets about doing so innovatively and with commendable courage.

She begins her argument by dismissing the idea that the 'received' concept of civil society — rule of law, voluntary social associations, human rights, and freedoms — can do anything for a world that has experienced deep collective trauma. Though universal values are essential for the constitution of citizenship; they are simply not enough to address contentious and intractable issues that bedevil transitions from conflict to post-conflict societies. Imposed norms howsoever universal and desirable they may be cannot contribute by themselves to the creation of mutual respect. People cannot be taught how to respect each other from the outside, or by appeals to values that are not part of their own memories. At some point the resources of a shared culture have to be excavated and tapped, and it is only then that the inheritors of this history can identify with the lessons of the past.

Though it is wise to borrow what is of value from other historical experiences so that one does not get caught up in solipsism, these values must necessarily be mediated by historically informed experiences. The components of a culture of civility have to be carefully and painfully assembled by tapping shared understandings, common memories, and historical experiences. The past is most definitely not another country; Gentile seems to suggest, it is integral to the present, providing a guide to roads taken and roads not taken, roads that should be taken and roads that should be avoided like the proverbial plague. But history can shed light on our current political predicaments only if we learn what is worth learning, and try and forget what is not choice worthy. As far as political projects are concerned, any reading of history must be selective.

Accordingly, if the paramount need of the time is to restore a shared culture of civility based on mutual respect and toleration for distinct and different ways of life and belief systems, there can be no better guide than the Millet system under the Ottoman Empire. The resurrection of the values of pluralism and mutual respect forms one strand of the culture of civility. The second strand is constituted by summoning up memories of what civil society meant to Bosnians laboring under Tito's militarized regime. In this particular context Bosnians had conceptualized civil society as the antithesis of a highly militarized regime; marked by interpersonal relations based on civility, warmth, dignity, respect, and toleration. If rich memories of the ways in which people of diverse persuasions could live together in harmony are articulated with universal values such as justice, we are encouraged to hope for a restoration of the culture of civility in a post-conflict society, holds Gentile.

The argument in this work summons up memories of the way a distinguished philosopher, and perhaps the first theorist who drew attention to the complexities of civil society, Hegel, tried to reconcile two contradictory trends in Germany in the early nineteenth century. It has generally been conceded that Hegel, a profound admirer of the Greek polis, was keen on recreating the spirit of wholeness and harmony found in ancient Athens in his *Philosophy of Right*. At the same time he knew that to attempt this would be not only be foolhardy, it was destined to fail. Nineteenth-century Germany was not ancient Greece. German society had been irremediably shaped by individuality, self-awareness and notions of individual rights and these values were not reconciled easily with the idea of a common good that could achieve perfectibility in society.

What Hegel did find in this welter of individualism, which if left alone might well threaten the existence of society itself, was a high degree of interdependence that had emerged as an interesting byproduct of intricate economic transactions. It is precisely here that he discovered the seeds of universality. It remained to reconcile the two dominant modes in which society understood itself, particularism in all its selfish detail, and universality. The space where the tension between the two could be worked out was civil society.

And this tension had to be worked out because civil society was an intermediate stage leading to the perfectly universal state embodying the *geist* of a social order. History had set out a unique task for Hegel's *burgerliche gesellschaft*; that of reconciling the moment of particularity or self-awareness so distinctive of modern human beings, and universality. But Hegel did not leave the task of reconciling this tension to contingency or to the exigencies of history; he organized civil society because the impulse to universality had to prevail over any other intention. There was no other option. Civil society, Hegel told us, is the theatre of history. But it cannot be left to itself; it might well explode. Anachronistically the precondition of the universal state is civil society but the state is also the precondition of civil society insofar as the latter needs to be organized in order to realize its historical task (Chandhoke 1995: chapter 4). I return to this point in the last paragraph of this argument.

Gentile, who relies heavily on the Hegelian conceptualization of civil society argues in the same strain that the historical task of civil society in post-conflict societies is to strive to create a culture of civility out of the universality as well as historical particularity. This is of enormous importance because a repeat performance of identity wars has to be forestalled. In the past, grievances, neither wholly real nor completely imaginary, had proved combustible in the hands of cultural war entrepreneurs. Their capacity to wreak havoc once again can only be neutralized if civil society performs the task allotted to it by history.

Gentile's argument is theoretically and politically important for one important reason. She suggests that no one model of civil society is going to work in every cultural and social context irrespective of history, linguistic conventions, and political practices. If we were to replace the language of rights with that of dignity, and if we were to think about the way universality can be mediated by historical specificities, we might be able to allot to the concept its rightful role in the social and political order. This is the precise message that needs to go out to international bureaucrats and policy makers who seek to reduce complex problems to a one-point agenda — create civil society. Civil society, Gentile reminds us, comes in different sizes and shapes, is forged through processes such as linguistic practices and historical experiences, and has to take on different tasks in specific historical experiences. By this argument alone she flattens out what passes for wisdom on how post-conflict societies can fashion a culture of living together.

The argument is well taken, but let me suggest that the rebuilding of a culture of civility, a task that has been handed down to civil society in post-conflict societies, might require another sort of cultural entrepreneur as well. The immediate job in a post-conflict society is not only one of excavating a culture of civility from shared histories, and restoring it as a necessary precondition for a public culture of democratic deliberation. The immediate job is to make sense of two kinds of histories of the society one prescribes for, a timeless history marked by respect for pluralism and toleration, and a recent history stamped with the cloven hoof of blood lust.

It seems to me that the two histories have to be brought face to face through cultural production, drama, poetry, art, literature, and popular culture such as films and music, contrasted and compared. I speak from the vantage point of northern India, a region that witnessed unimaginable scenes of horror when the country was partitioned in 1947. The partition bore dreadful consequences in the shape of involuntary mass migrations, ethnic cleansing, gang rapes, and sordid mutilations, all of which have left vivid scars upon the memories of populations on both sides of the border. The twentieth century is known for the violence that was unleashed during two world wars, liberation wars, and proxy wars. Even by these standards the partition of India stands out for the sheer carnage that destroyed people and their memories of living together. An estimated one million people were killed in brutal encounters, and half these deaths took place in the region of the Punjab. In another historical context, A. E. Housman (1940: 155) had written: 'They say my verse is sad: no wonder, Its narrow measure spans, Tears of eternity and sorrow, Not mine, but man's.' These lines may well provide the epigraph of ethnonationalist conflict.

Over time, people on both sides of the border of Punjab found that the best way to heal wounds was through rediscovering and reviving the magic of a shared culture. Determined efforts to recreate shared history through music concerts, theatre and rendering of folk music have slowly but surely brought people across territorial borders together in a shared project, that of recreating a common regional culture and language. A culture of civility has been slowly and painfully constructed out of the rubble of shared history through cultural production.

Gramsci had spoken about civil society as the space for the production and reproduction of hegemonic values, but also as the site where cultural projects can counteract hegemony. In that way Gramsci followed Hegel rather than Marx in his conceptualization of civil society. There is no essence to civil society, civil society is a project of many projects, a space where rival and conflicting narratives about the past, the shape of the future, and an analysis of the present are juxtaposed. This really implies that civil society is itself conflictual; constantly divided between, say, democratic and antidemocratic groups and their agendas. How democratic groups go about pursuing their agenda of restoring a culture of civility depends on their imagination, the reach of their vision, the state-of-the-art techniques they bring to bear upon the task, their powers of persuasion, their capacity to move hearts and minds and above all their readiness to counter anti-democratic agendas with patience, with a fair degree of toleration here and some amount of intolerance there. Gentile agrees that civil society can often be as polarized as political society, and that it becomes even more difficult to distinguish a segment of civil society that reflects the same form of divisiveness that characterizes the state. She understands the pitfalls but perhaps underestimates the power of narratives of victimhood.

In Julian Barnes' Booker award–winning novel, *A Sense of An Ending*, the narrator, Tony Webster, reminds us that history is not only the lies of the victors but also the self-delusions of the vanquished. It is conceivable that self-delusions will continue to grip the collective psyche. In such cases, not only coming to grips with the recent past, but also engaging each other in a project of restoring a culture of civility demands that a cultural entrepreneur should be able to draw upon a stock of infinite resources, energies, and commitment.

Yet dangers remain. Of course we should look at the internal resources of a society, and see how these can be tapped before offering a ready-made solution to some very intractable problems. This makes for good common sense. Gentile argues that in the past the culture of civility was woven out of two strands, the historical lessons learnt from the Millet system, and the definition of civil society in opposition to a highly militarized state structure.

A number of theorists in India have argued that instead of institutionalizing secularism as a defining characteristic of a state in a religious society, we should summon resources of toleration that were the signpost of plural societies learning how to live together. It is true that toleration of different belief systems was a property of social relations in pre-modern times. But we also have to recollect Ernst Gellner's warning that 'culturally plural societies worked well in the past', but 'genuine cultural pluralism ceases to be viable under current conditions' (Gellner 1983: 55). Paramount among these current conditions is competition in two predominant realms, the market and public office. In such circumstances toleration can no longer emerge from the adage that group x should do things its own way, and group y should do so in its own way, and never the twain shall meet. People cannot afford to leave each other alone when the stakes are so high.

In such a society, philosophical grounds for toleration have to be reworked; they cannot be based on indifference and lack of interaction, which may be symptomatic of a premarket society. When people do not engage with each other, we do not require toleration. But such circumstances are precluded by the demands of modern society. Who our children go to school with, who we meet in our professional capacities, which religious persuasion the candidate who asks for our votes belongs to, what are the codes that govern the project of living together — secularism or theocracy — have deep implications on the way we live our lives. It is precisely because our paths, our careers, our lives impact others, as much as others lives impact us, that the concept of toleration becomes of dominating importance. And it is precisely for this reason that toleration becomes sometimes an impossible dream. This brings me to the second aspect of rebuilding a culture of civility argued for by Gentile.

She writes that civil society in Bosnia was distinctive insofar as it distanced itself from the militarized state that had been established by Tito. This is typical of the way civil societies developed in Central and Eastern Europe in the 1980s, in abstraction from the state, in opposition to the state and its overwhelming logic of power. But when democracy has been restored, can civil society afford to turn its back on the state and concentrate on the building of a culture of civility? It cannot afford to do this for two reasons. One, it is simply not enough to restore historically fashioned understandings to the centre-stage of a political project. Of course toleration and respect for pluralism is important as a core component of a culture of civility. But at some point this norm has to be legislated, implemented, and protected against those who would challenge the norm itself. This means that civil society has to engage with the state and see that the culture of civility it has fashioned is established as a political norm.

Certainly, the concept of civil society specifies that associational life in a metaphorical space between the household, the market, and the state is valuable in itself. Associational life neutralizes the individualism, the atomism, and the anomie that modernity brings in its wake. Social associations by bringing people together in multiple projects such as a culture of civility as Gentile suggests, engender and nurture solidarity and empathy. The projects themselves might range from developing popular consciousness about climate change, to discussing and dissecting popular culture, to supporting needy children, to organizing neighborhood activities. Or projects might simply intend to enhance sociability and dissipate alienation. It does not matter. Whatever be the specific reason why people get together; for a determinate purpose or for mere sociability, associational life is an intrinsic good.

Associational life is a good in another sense inasmuch as networks of associations facilitate collective action. And participation in collective action enables the realization of human agency insofar as citizens recognize and appreciate that they possess the right to take part in decision-making, and that they possess the competence to do so. In other words, collective action brings to fruition the basic presumption of democracy — popular sovereignty.

Second, though associational life is of value in its own right, if we de-link this aspect of civil society from the struggle for citizenship rights, the state might be let off the hook. Why is not letting the state off the hook important? The one idea that arguably lies at the heart of the civil society argument is that states that claim to be democratic are likely to be imperfectly so. Democracy is a project that has to be realized through collective action as well as sustained engagement with the state. Citizen activism, public vigilance, informed public opinion, a free media, and a multiplicity of social associations are necessary preconditions for this task. For these reasons and more, civil society simply cannot afford to define itself in opposition to the state. Civil society as a project of projects is the space of deliberation and debate on the kind of society that exists and how it can be transformed. But at some level it has to engage with the state. In the Hegelian sense it has to be the precondition of the state but the state also has to be the precondition of civil society.

Therefore, even though civil society in Bosnia has to take on the crucial task of recapturing and reinstating the culture of civility at the heart of political thinking, it has to go further. It has to take on the state, it has to campaign to translate this culture of civility into law, and it has to realize thereby democracy. The culture of civility elaborated so lucidly by Gentile has to be institutionalized both in civil society and in the state.

A reply to Professor Chandhoke
Culture of civility and pluralism: the 'institutional problem'

The notion of civil society has a great conceptual and theoretical power. This is what I realized when I first approached this topic as a young Ph.D. candidate. As Hegel suggested, 'the creation of civil society is the achievement of the modern world', but this link with modernity is complex and, sometimes, ambivalent. The capitalist economy and the development of the modern nation-state led intellectuals to find new spaces and ways of accommodating individuals' interests and aspirations in such a complex society. If the idea of civil society came to dominate the debates since the Scottish Enlightenment, only with Hegel a systematic formulation that could grasp the complexity of this notion was elaborated. Hegel was the first to recognize that in modern societies citizens' autonomy was deeply challenged by two different sources of power, the market and the state. Civil society became, then, the territory of mediation between the private and the public, governmental institutions and free market. It is this tension between public and private, between collective aspirations and the atomistic dimension of the modern capitalist society that enriched this concept of new nuances over the years.

Yet, there is a distance between different theoretical interpretations of civil society and the empirical dimension of its movements and organizations. In her inspiring commentary, Professor Chandhoke invites the reader to reflect upon some relevant issues concerning the notion of civil society and the idea of culture of civility related to it. By civil society structures and associations we mostly refer to a variegated world of different actors and organizations. It therefore includes both those segmented groups whose membership is strictly ascribed, like ethnic or religious groups, and more fluid voluntary associations organized around different values or topics, like environmental associations, workers' groups, interest groups, etc.[1] Civil society often results, therefore, as polarized and ambivalent as the political society. In particular, as I have emphasized on many occasions in this book, this ambivalent character of civil society becomes evident in the aftermath of an ethno-religious conflict, when frustrated identities and the memory of the past violence come into place. As Professor Chandhoke notes, if it is true that civil society as 'a project of projects' presupposes the state, it is also true that the state has to be the precondition for civil society. In this sense, the idea of 'culture of civility' might have some impact on the future democratic transition of a deeply divided society only if it is actually incorporated into a legal normative framework.

Professor Chandhoke, thus, warns us regarding two somehow related problems linked to the notion of civil society. First, she is suspicious about the sort of pluralism of identities and organizations which characterizes civil society. In other words, when civil society is heavily segmented along identity lines it becomes a crucial field of political and social confrontation for the recognition. If this is so, the sort of consensus emerging at the level of civil society has to be an institutional one. Chandhoke says, 'of course toleration and respect for pluralism is important as a core component of a culture of civility. But at some point this norm has to be legislated, implemented, and protected against those who would challenge the norm itself. [....] Civil society has to engage with the state and see that the culture of civility it has fashioned is established as a political norm.' For the sake of argument, I distinguish two parts of Chandhoke's comment. The first part is concerned with the problem of the role of identity and how this can be handled within civil society associations and organizations. I will then come back to the second 'institutional problem'.

From a liberal viewpoint, I am prone to consider the distinction between public and private sphere as a crucial one in the development of the contemporary formulation of civil society. Liberal institutions, that are based on values such as neutrality, liberty and equality, are meant to offer a legal framework which regulates and differentiates among individuals' public and private life. The boundary between civil society and government reflects therefore this crucial distinction. Civil society — as presented in this book — is in fact the space for pluralism of identities where values, beliefs and private interests emerge and individuals have the experience of tolerating and dealing with diversity. This terrain of plural and particularistic identities is opposed to that of the unity represented by the government with its overarching legal and institutional framework. In this book, I put a great emphasis on what I call the 'experience of pluralism' individuals make at the level of civil society: through associational life individuals experience plural memberships, they recognize the plurality of their identities and different modes of identification. This is especially true in the case of voluntary associations, where membership is consensual and exit possible. This characteristic of civil society represents the precondition of what I call the 'culture of civility.' Yet,

Professor Chandhoke tells us that this can be highly problematic in deeply divided societies. In these contexts, associational life is often highly segmented along ethnic or religious identities. In these cases, group identification and loyalty might hamper the possibility to experience other forms of identifications. These groups are often characterized by restricted membership and illiberal practices. In some way, what Chandhoke is arguing is that the senses of toleration and reciprocity linked to the 'culture of civility' might emerge and work in practice only in a society which has already incorporated liberal practices and values. In this case the contextual and historical integrates the institutional universal system of norms. Yet, in societies deeply divided along ethno-religious lines, the practice of toleration should be translated into the normative legal framework. This process implies that it is not enough to recognize decent practices that have some sort of historical tradition as a mere *modus vivendi*. Institutions should in fact incorporate a liberal principle of toleration as a crucial political one and citizens should recognize it for the 'right reasons'.

The issue raised by Professor Chandhoke is a very important one. In the last years, the most relevant criticisms raised towards the idea of culture of civility were somehow linked to this issue: the idea of culture of civility seems to underestimate actual polarizations and potential conflicts emerging at the level of civil society before and after an ethno-religious conflict. In the Conclusion, I have shown how the idea of culture of civility responds to the challenge coming from the debate on the so-called 'bad civil society'. In addition, I clarified that the idea of culture of civility does not disregard the existence of deep divisions within societies, neither does it assume that a climate of trust and tolerance has always existed before the ethnic or religious tensions. I am quite prone to admit that the notion of civil society implies a plurality of actors and associational modalities that range from fluid, plural and voluntary associations to forms of sectarianism and rigid segmentation. Yet, it is difficult to distinguish rigidly fluid societies from segmented societies: in any civil society voluntary and ascribed associations, open and closed groups are represented even though in different proportions (Rosenblum and Post 2002: 4). Chandhoke is right when she argues that not only history but also the existing legal norms allow the identities affirmed in civil society to develop and accept values such as toleration and respect. However, as I often argue in this book, identity itself it is not a static concept. The ascriptive identities which are often emphasized in some groups are not the whole of individual identity. In fact, it is not the effective belonging to a specific group which makes possible the emergence of a culture of civility, it is rather the experience of being part of an association and the recognition of the plurality of experiences within and out of the association that constitute the basis of the civility and the self-respect. Rightly, Post and Rosenblum have noted that 'every component of civil society, even hermetic separatist communities, are permeable to the influence of the other group, to the overarching public culture, to influences from abroad, and to the ceaseless invention of novel values and social forms' (ibid.).

The idea of culture of civility, in this sense, serves to define the *thin* form of public reasoning that takes place at the societal level. It is located inbetween the two levels of the unmitigated pluralism of the 'background culture' and the reasonable pluralism of the overarching public political culture. However, it includes both in a specific way: it is rooted in the historical and the contextual, but it introduces and anticipates values such as self-respect and reciprocity that enable individuals to articulate discussions and judgements which can be accepted by others. This culture can range from a 'thin' kind of procedural decency (making agreement in good faith, refusal of violence in public space), to the thickest forms of civility in which common substantive norms (as respect for differences, toleration, condemnation of racist rules) are accepted.

The example of the associations of victims that emerged in Bosnia becomes then relevant to show how it is possible to move from segmented to fluid civil societies. These associations are strictly defined in sectarian terms affiliations and the 'narratives of victim-hood', to use Chandhoke's words, can be a very divisive one. However, a dramatic story of raping or torture in a Bosnian village can be told in terms of the guilt of a specific ethnic group, but it can also be seen as a violation of basic principles which apply to all human beings. Moreover, the inclusion of victims' more or less formal deliberative forums, as those promoted by the ICMP, offers them a political opportunity to act as citizens, in this way delegitimizing ethno-political divisions.[2]

However, a further clarification must be provided regarding what I called the 'institutional problem'. Civil society is the sphere of pluralism where particular interests and collective aspirations co-exist. However, it is equally true that the forms of civility and decency which characterize civil society are possible only if they find actual implementation within the legal institutional frame-work. In this respect, Walzer has famously argued that civil society 'requires political agency' (Walzer 2003: 79): the state with its legal normative framework balances particularism and pluralism, encourages associationism and protects individuals' freedom and rights. As I said before, in contrast to the pluralism and particularity of the civil society the legal institutional framework constitutes the unity and the common identity of a political community. However, in deeply divided societies, newly emerged institutional settlements are the product of hard negotiations, which very often reflect the deep divisions that emerged during the war. Frequently, the major challenge to the democratization process is in fact related to the absence of an actual political community and the sense of citizenship is deeply undermined by the memory of offences like genocides and ethnic cleansings.

In this sense, Chandhoke's point regarding the relevance of institutions is a very crucial one. Inclusive and pluralistic civil society and liberal democracy are reciprocally supportive. However, if many scholars tend to agree that liberal democratic institutions are the precondition for a democratic and inclusive civil society, they often underestimate the role of civil society in shaping liberal and tolerant institutions. The idea of a culture of civility presented in this book aims to bring political theorists to consider also this second aspect as a response to ethnic or religious violence and as a precondition to restore civility in deeply divided societies. The public recognition of values emerging from the societal level can be of some support to foster reconciliation and democratic transition in divided societies. Especially in contexts where governments are weak and a 'genuine public identity' is fragile, the social cooperation is legitimated by a social contract, that can range from a modus vivendi to forms of moral consensus, among competing groups and associations. The idea of culture of civility anticipates therefore the process of principled reasoning for cooperation embodied by a strong public reason. However, the democratic transition and the process of reconciliation in these societies crucially depend on the capacity of the institutions to restore a 'common moral horizon' incorporating in the legal normative framework those values emerging from the culture of civility.

NOTES

1. On this, see also Rosenblum and Post   2. On this, see chapter 4.
(2002: 3–4).

Bibliography

Aall, P. 2001. 'What Do NGOs Bring to Peace-making?' in: *Turbulent Peace: The Challenges of Managing International Conflict* (edited by C. Crocker, F. O. Hampson and P. Aall). United States Institute of Peace Press, Washington, D.C., pp. 365–84.

———— 2007. 'The Power of Nonofficial Actors in Conflict Management', in: *Leashing the Dogs of War: Conflict Management in a Divided World* (edited by C. Crocker, F. O. Hampson and P. Aall). United States Institute of Peace Press, Washington D.C., pp. 477–94.

Amnesty International. 2003. '"Bosnia-Herzegovina": Shelving Justice — War Crimes Prosecutions In Paralysis', Amnesty International Index, EUR 63/018/2003, 12 November, http://www.unhcr.org/refworld/docid/402f85be4.html (accessed 11 May 2011).

Andreas, P. 2004. 'The Clandestine Political Economy of War and Peace in Bosnia'. *International Studies Quarterly* 48: 29–51.

Anheier, H. E. 2000. 'Managing Non-Profit Organizations: Toward a New Approach', in: LSE CCS Working Papers Collection, n. 1, London.

Anheier, H. E. and M. Albrow. 2007. 'Violence and the Possibility of Civility', in: *Global Civil Society Yearbook 2006-7* (edited by H. E. Anheier, M. Kaldor and M. Glasius). Oxford University Press, Oxford, 1-15.

Anheier, H. E. and Y. R. Isar. 2007. *Conflicts and Tensions.* Sage, London.

Anheier, H. E., M. Kaldor and M. Glasius (eds). 2001. *Global Civil Society Yearbook 2001.* Oxford University Press, Oxford.

———— 2006. *Global Civil Society Yearbook 2006–7.* Oxford University Press, Oxford.

Appiah, A. K. 2007. *The Ethics of Identity.* Princeton University Press, New Jersey.

Aral, B. 2004. 'The Idea of Human Rights as Perceived in the Ottoman Empire'. *Human Rights Quarterly* 26: 454–82.

Arendt, H. 1958. *The Human Condition.* University of Chicago Press, Chicago.

Arkoun, M. 2002. 'Locating Civil Society in Islamic Contexts', in: *Civil Society in the Muslim World, Contemporary Perspectives* (edited by A. B. Sajoo). Tauris Publishers, London, 35-60.

Ayoob, M. 1996. 'State-making, State-breaking and State Failure', in: *Between Development and Destruction* (edited by L. Van De Goor, K. Rupesinghe and P. Sciarone). Palgrave, London, pp. 67–86.

Azar, E. E. 1972. 'Conflict Escalation and Conflict Reduction in an International Crisis: Suez, 1956'. *The Journal of Conflict Resolution* 16: 183–201.

———— 1990. 'Protracted Social Conflict: An Analytical Frame-work', in: *The Management of Protracted Social Conflicts: Theory and Cases* (edited by E. E. Azar). Dartmouth, Aldershot, pp. 5–17.

———— 1991. 'The Analysis and Management of Protracted Social Conflict', in: *The Psychodynamics of International Relationships* (edited by J. Volkan J. Montville and D. Julius). D.C. Heath, Lexington, KY, pp. 93–120.

Azar, E. E., P. Jureidini and R. Mclaurin. 1978. 'Protracted Social Conflict; Theory and Practice in the Middle East'. *Journal of Palestine Studies* 8: 41–60.

Barnett, J. 2008. 'Peace and Development: Towards a New Synthesis'. *Annual Review of Sociology* 45: 75–89.

Bates, T. 1975. 'Gramsci and the Theory of Hegemony'. *Journal of the History of Ideas* 36: 351–366.

Beck, U. 2002. 'The Cosmopolitan Society and Its Enemies'. *Theory Culture Society* 19: 17–44.

Bellamy, A. J. 2002. 'The Great Beyond: Rethinking Military Responses to New Wars and Complex Emergencies'. *Defence Studies* 2: 25–50.

Belloni, R. 2001. 'Civil Society and Peacebuilding in Bosnia and Herzegovina'. *Annual Review of Sociology* 38: 163–80.

———— 2008. 'Civil Society in War-to-Democracy Transitions', in: *From War-to-Democracy Transitions: Dilemmas of Democratization and Peace-Building in War Societies* (edited by Anna Jarstard and Timothy Sisk). Cambridge: Cambridge University Press, pp. 182–210.

Bennett, P. 2007. 'The Media and the War: Seeing the Human', in: *Open Democracy*, available at http://www.opendemocracy.net/article/media_net/journalism_war/media_war_seeing_human (accessed 14 January 2013).

Berrebi, C. 2009. 'The Economics of Terrorism and Counterterrorism: What Matters and is Rational-Choice Theory Helpful?' in: *Social Science for Counterterrorism: Putting the Pieces Together* (edited by P. K. Davis and K. Cragin). Santa Monica, CA: RAND, pp. 151–208.

Bieber, F. 2002. 'Aid Dependency in Bosnian Politics and Civil Society: Failures and Successes of Post-war Peacebuilding in Bosnia-Herzegovina'. *Croatian International Relations Review* 8 (26/27): 25–29.

———— 2004. 'Institutionalizing Ethnicity in the Western Balkans Managing Change in Deeply Divided Societies'. ECMI Working Paper 19.

Bisogno, M. and A. Chong. 2002. 'Poverty and Inequality in Bosnia and Herzegovina After the Civil War'. *World Development* 30: 61–75.

Bobbio, N. 1988. 'Gramsci and the Concept of Civil Society', in: *Civil Society and the State: New European Perspectives* (edited by J. Keane). Verso, London, pp. 73–99.

Bojkov, V. D. 2003. 'Democracy in Bosnia and Herzegovina: Post-1995 Political System and its Functioning'. *Southeast European Politics* 4: 41–67.

Bougarel, X. 1996. *Bosnie: anatomie d'un conflit*. La Découverte, Paris.

———— 1999. 'Yugoslav Wars: The "Revenge of the Countryside": Between Sociological Reality and Nationalist Myth'. *East European Quarterly* 33: 157.

Bougarel, X., E. Helms and G. Duijzings. 2007. *The New Bosnian Mosaic. Identities, Memories and Moral Claims in a Post-War Society*. Ashgate, London.

Brubaker, R. 2004. 'Ethnicity Without Group', in: *Facing Ethnic Conflicts: Toward a New Realism* (edited by A. Wimmer, R. J. Goldstone, D. L. Horowitz, U. Joras and C. Schetter). Rowman & Littlefield Publishers, INC, Oxford, 34-52.

Brubaker, R. and D. D. Laitin. 1998. 'Ethnic and Nationalist Violence'. *Annual Review of Sociology* 24: 423–52.

Callahan, D. 1998. *Unwinnable Wars: American Power and Ethnic Conflict*. Hill and Wang, New York.

Campbell, D. 2002. 'Atrocity, Memory, Photography: Imaging the Concentration Camps of Bosnia — The Case of ITN versus Living Marxism, Part 2'. *Journal of Human Rights* 1: 143–72.

Carlson, M. and O. Listhaug. 2007. 'Citizens' Perceptions of Human Rights Practices: An Analysis of 55 Countries'. *Annual Review of Sociology* 44: 465–83.

Chambers S. 2002. 'A Critical Theory of Civil Society', in: *Alternative Conceptions of Civil Society* (edited by S. Chambers and W. Kymlicka.). Princeton University Press, Princeton, N.J., pp. 90–110.

Chambers, S. and J. Kopstein. 2001. 'Bad Civil Society'. *Political Theory* 29 (2001): 837–65.

Chandhoke, Neera. 1995. *State and Civil Society: Explorations in Political Theory*. Sage, New Delhi.

————. 2005. 'What the Hell Is "Civil Society"?' in: *Open Democracy*, available at http://www.opendemocracy.net/democracy-open_politics/article_2375.jsp (accessed 14 January 2013).

Charney, C. 1999. 'Civil Society, Political Violence, and Democratic Transitions: Business and the Peace Process in South Africa, 1990 to 1994'. *Comparative Studies in Society and History* 41: 182–206.

Chatterjee, P. 2001. 'On Civil and Political Society in Postcolonial Democracies', in: *Civil Society: History and Possibilities* (edited by S. Kaviraj and S. Khilnani). Cambridge University Press, Cambridge, pp. 165–78.

Clausewitz, K. V. 1989. 'On War', in: *On War, Wordsworth Classics of World Literature* (edited and translated by M. E. Howard, P. Paret). Wordsworth Editions, Kent, UK.

Cohen J. 2006. 'Is There a Human Rights to Democracy?' in *The Egalitarian Conscience: Essays in Honour of G. A. Cohen* (edited by Christine Sypnowich). Oxford University Press, Oxford, pp. 226–48. Chapter available at http://iisdb.stanford.edu/pubs/21328/is_there_a_human_right_to_democracy.pdf (accessed 20 May 2008).

Cohen, J. and A. Arato. 1994. *Civil Society and Political Theory*. MIT Press, Cambridge, MA.

Collier, P. 2007. 'Economic Causes of Civil Conflict and Their Implications for Policy', in: *Leashing the Dogs of the War* (edited by C. Crocker, F. O. Hampson and P. Aall). United States Institute of Peace Press, Washington, D.C., pp. 197–218.

Collier, P. and A. Hoeffler. 2004. 'Greed and Grievance in Civil War'. *Oxf. Econ. Pap.* 56: 563–95.

Collier P., A. Hoeffler and M. Söderbom. 2006. 'Aid, Policies and Risk in Post-Conflict Societies', in: Working Paper Collection, Centre for the Study of African Economies. University of Oxford, Oxford.

Comaroff J. and J. Comaroff (eds). 1999. *Civil Society and the Political Imagination in Africa*. University Press, Chicago.

Cox, M. 2003. 'Building Democracy from Outside. The Dayton Agreement in Bosnia & Herzegovina', in: *Can Democracy Be Designed? The Politics and Institutional Choice in Conflict-Torn Societies* (edited by S. Bastian and R. Luckham). Zed Books, London, pp. 253–76.

Cox, R. W. 1999. 'Civil Society at the Turn of the Millennium: Prospects for Alternative World Order'. *Review of International Studies* 25: 3–28.

Crawford, B. 2007. 'Globalization and Cultural Conflict: An Institutional Approach', in: *Conflicts and Tensions* (edited by H. E. Anheier and Y. R. Isar). Sage, London, pp. 31–51.

Dahl, R. A. 2000. 'A Democratic Paradox?' *Political Science Quarterly* 115: 35–40.

Delpla, I. 2007. 'In the Midst of Injustice: The ICTY from the Perspective of Some Victim Associations', in: *The New Bosnian Mosaic: Identities, Memories and Moral Claims in a Post-War Society* (edited by X. Bougarel, E. Helms and G. Duijzings). Ashgate, London, pp. 211–34.

Diamond, L. J. 2005. 'Lessons from Iraq'. *Journal of Democracy* 16: 9–23.

Donia, R. J. and J. V. A. Fine, Jr. 1994. *Bosnia-Hercegovina: A Tradition Betrayed*. Hurst & Company, London.

Donnelly, J. 1982. 'Human Rights and Human Dignity: An Analytic Critique of Non-Western Human Rights Conception'. *Political Science Review* 76: 303–16.

———— 1984. 'Cultural Relativism and Universal Human Rights'. *Human Rights Quarterly* 6: 400–419.

———— 2003. *Universal Human Rights in Theory and Practice*. Cornell University Press, New York.

———— 2007a. *International Human Rights* (Dilemmas in World Politics). Westview Press, Boulder.

———— 2007b. 'The Relative Universality of Human Rights'. *Human Rights Quarterly* 29: 281–306.

———— 2009. 'Human Dignity and Human Rights', Research Project on Human Dignity, Swiss Initiative to Commemorate the 60th Anniversary of the UDHR. Available at http://www.udhr60.ch/report/donnelly-HumanDignity_0609.pdf (accessed 30 January 2013).

Dryzek, J. S. 2005. 'Deliberative Democracy in Divided Societies: Alternatives to Agonism and Analgesia'. *Political Theory* 33(2): 218–42.

Dryzeck, J. S. and S. Niemeyer. 2006. 'Reconciling Pluralism and Consensus as Political Ideals'. *American Journal of Political Science* 50 (3): 634–49.

Duffield, M. 1998. 'Post-modern Conflict: Warlords, Post-adjustment States and Private Protection'. *Civil Wars* 1: 65–102.

———— 2001. *Global Governance and the New Wars*. Zed Books, London.

———— 2002. 'Social Reconstruction and the Radicalization of Development: Aid as a Relation of Global Liberal Governance'. *Development and Change* 33: 1049–71.

Eberle, C. J. 2002. *Religious Conviction in Liberal Politics*. Cambridge University Press, Cambridge.

Edwards, M. 2004. *Civil Society*. Polity, Cambridge.

Enterline, A. J. and G. J. Michael. 2008. 'The History of Imposed Democracy and the Future of Iraq and Afghanistan'. *Foreign Policy Analysis* 4: 321–47.

Eriksson, M., P. Wallensteen and M. Sollenberg. 2003. 'Armed Conflict, 1989–2002'. *Annual Review of Sociology* 40: 593–607.

Falk, R. 1995. *On Humane Governance: Towards a New Global Politics*. Pennsylvania State University Press, University Park, Penn.

———— 2002. 'Trends towards Transnational Justice: Innovations and Institutions', in: *Human Development Report 2002*. UNDP Human Development Report Office.

Fearon, J. D. 2005. 'Primary Commodity Exports and Civil War'. *Journal of Conflict Resolution* 49: 483–507.

Fearon, J. D. and D. D. Laitin. 2003. 'Ethnicity, Insurgency, and Civil War'. *American Political Science Review* 97: 1–16.

Ferguson, A. 1767. *An Essay on the History of Civil Society* (edited by F. Oz-Salzberger). Cambridge University Press, Cambridge.

Fetherston, B. 1999. 'The Transformative Potential of NGOs: The Centre for Peace Studies in Croatia'. *NGOs in the Field of International Peace and Security: Problems and Perspectives* 12: 10–12.

Fischer, M. 2006. 'Civil Society in Conflict Transformation: Ambivalence, Potential and Challenges' (Berlin: Berghof Research Center, www.berghof-handbook.net, Oct. 2006). Available at http://www.berghof-handbook.net/documents/publications/fischer_cso_handbook.pdf (accessed 30 January 2013).

Flottau R. and M. Kraske. 2005. 'Apartheid in Bosnia', in: Der Spiegel, November 7. Available at http://www.spiegel.de/international/spiegel/dayton-10-years-on-apartheid-in-bosnia-a-383962.html (accessed 30 January 2013).

Foley, M. W. and B. Edwards. 1996. 'The Paradox of Civil Society'. *Journal of Democracy* 7: 38–52.

Foucault, M. 2003. *Society Must Be Defended.*

Lectures at the College de France, 1975–1976. St. Martin's Press, New York.

Frost, M. 2002. *Constituting Human Rights: Global Civil Society and the Society of Democratic State*. Routledge, London.

Fukuyama, F. 1992. *The End of History and the Last Man*. Free Press, New York.

——— 1999. *Social Capital and Civil Society*. The Institute of Public Policy, George Mason University.

Galtung, J. 1969. 'Violence, Peace and Peace Research'. *Annual Review of Sociology* 3: 167–92.

——— 1990. 'Cultural Violence'. Annual Review of Sociology 27: 291–305.

——— 1996. 'Conflict Formations', in: *Peace by Peaceful Means: Peace and Conflict, Development and Civilization* (edited by PRIO). Sage Publications, London, 70-80.

Gellner, E. 1983, *Nations and Nationalisms*. Basil Blackwell, Oxford.

Gramsci, A. 1910–26. *Selection from the Prison Notebooks* (edited by Q. Hoare and G. Nowell-Smith). Lawrence & Wishart, London.

Guelke, A., 2012. *Politics in Deeply Divided Societies*. Polity, London.

Gurr, T. R. 1994. 'Peoples against the State: Ethno-political Conflict in the Changing World System'. *International Studies Quarterly* 38: 347–77.

——— 2001. 'Minorities and Nationalists: Managing Ethno-political Conflict in the New Century', in: *Turbulent Peace: The Challenges of Managing International Conflict* (edited by C. Crocker, F. O. Hampson and P. Aall). United States Institute of Peace Press, Washington, D.C., pp. 163–88.

——— 2007. 'Minorities, Nationalists, and Islamists: Managing Communal Conflicts in the Twenty-First Century', in: *Leashing the Dogs of War: Conflict Management in a Divided World* (edited by C. A. Crocker et al.). US Institute of Peace Press, Washington, D.C., pp. 131–60.

Gurr T. R., M. Woodward and M. Marshall. 2005. 'Forecasting Instability: Are Ethnic Wars and Muslim Countries Different?' in: *Proceedings of the 2005 Annual Meeting of the American Political Science Association*, 1–4 September.

Habermas, J. 1989. *The Structural Transformation of the Public Sphere: An Inquiry into a Category of Bourgeois Society* (Studies in Contemporary German Social Thought). MIT Press, Cambridge, Mass.

——— 1996. *Between Facts and Norms: Contribution to a Discourse Theory of Law and Democracy*. MIT Press, Cambridge, Mass.

——— 2001. *Post-national Constellation*. MIT Press, Cambridge, Mass.

Hartzell, Caroline, Matthew Hoddi and Donald Rothchild. 2001. 'Stabilizing Peace after Civil War: An Investigation of Some Key Variables'. *International Organization* 92(3): 183–208.

Hegel, G.W.F. 1996. *Philosophy of Right* (Translated by S.W. Dyde). Prometheus Books, Amherst, N.Y.

Held, D. 1995. *Democracy and Global Order. From the Modern State to Cosmopolitan Governance*. Polity Press, Cambridge.

Helms, E. 2007. '"Politics is a Whore": Women, Morality and Victimhood in Post-War Bosnia & Herzegovina', in: *The New Bosnian Mosaic: Identities, Memories and Moral Claims in a Post-War Society* (edited by X. Bougarel, E. Helms and G. Duijzings). Ashgate, London, pp. 235–54.

Hobbes, T. 1668. *The Leviathan* (edited by C. B. Macpherson). Penguin, Harmondsworth, Middlesex, UK.

Horowitz, D. L. 1998. 'Structure and Strategy in Ethnic Conflict', in: World Bank Conference on Development Economics. World Bank, Washington, D.C.

——— 2001. *Ethnic Groups in Conflict*. University of California Press, Berkeley, CA.

Housman, A. E. 1940. *The Collected Poems of A.E. Housman*. Henry Holt and Co., New York.

Humanrightswatch. 1992. 'War Crimes in Bosnia Hercegovina': A Helsinki Watch Report. Human Rights Watch, New York.

Huntington, S. P. 1991. *The Third Wave: Democratization in the Late Twentieth Century*. University of Oklahoma Press, Norman.

———— 1993. 'The Clash of Civilizations?' *Foreign Affairs* 72: 22–49.

———— 1996. *The Clash of Civilizations and the Remaking of World Order*. Simon & Schuster, New York.

Hutchinson J. 1994. 'Cultural Nationalism and Moral Regeneration', in: *Nationalism* (edited by J. Hutchinson). Oxford University Press, Oxford, pp. 122–31.

———— 1996. *Ethnicity*. Oxford University Press, Oxford.

Hutchinson, J. and A. Smith. 1994. *Nationalism*. Oxford University Press, Oxford.

ICG. 2000. 'War Criminals in Bosnia's Republika Srpska: Who Are People in Your Neighbourhood?' (edited by ICG). ICG, Brussels/Sarajevo.

———— 2002a. 'Implementing Equality: The "Constituent Peoples" Decision in Bosnia & Herzegovina' (edited by International Crisis Group). ICG, Brussels/Sarajevo. Available at http://www.crisisgroup.org/~/media/Files/europe/Bosnia%2045 (accessed 30 January 2013).

———— 2002b. 'The Continuing Challenge of Refugee Return in Bosnia & Herzegovina' (edited by International Crisis Group). ICG, Brussels/Sarajevo. Available at http://www.crisisgroup.org/~/media/Files/europe/137%20-%20The%20Continuing%20Challenge%20Of%20Refugee%2 0Return%20In%20Bosnia (accessed 30 January 2013).

Ignatieff, M. 1993. *Blood and Belonging: Journeys into the New Nationalism*. BBC Books, London.

———— 1997. *The Warrior's Honor: Ethnic War and the Modern Conscience*. Henry Holt & Co, LLC, New York.

———— 2003. *Empire Lite: Nation Building in Bosnia, Kosovo, Afghanistan*. Vintage, London.

Jovanovich, M. A. 2005. 'Recognising Minority Identities through Collective Rights'. *Human Rights Quarterly* 27: 625–51.

Kaldor, M. 1999. *New and Old Wars: Organised Violence in a Global Era*. Polity, Cambridge.

———— 2002. 'Civil Society and Accountability', in: *Human Development Report 2002*. UNDP Human Development Report Office.

———— 2003a. *Global Civil Society: An Answer to War*. Polity, Cambridge.

———— 2003b. 'The Idea of Global Civil Society'. *International Affairs* 79: 583–93.

———— 2004. 'Nationalism and Globalisation'. *Nations and Nationalism* 10: 161–77.

———— 2005. 'Old Wars, Cold Wars, New Wars, and the War on Terror'. *International Politics* 42: 491–98.

Kaldor, M., D. Kostovikova and Y. Said. 2007. 'War and Peace: The Role of Global Civil Society', in: *Global Civil Society Yearbook 2006/2007* (edited by H. E. Anheier, M. Kaldor and M. Glasius). Sage, London, pp. 94–119.

Kaldor, M. and D. Muro. 2003. 'Religious and Nationalist Militant Groups', in: *Global Civil Society Yearbook 2003* (edited by H. E. Anheier, M. Kaldor and M. Glasius). Oxford University Press, Oxford, pp. 151–83.

Kalyvas, S. N. 2001. '"New" and "Old" Civil Wars: A Valid Distinction?' *World Politics* 54: 99–118.

———— 2003. 'The Ontology of "Political Violence": Action and Identity in Civil Wars". *Perspectives on Politics* 1: 475–94.

———— 2007. 'Ethnic Cleavages and Irregular War: Iraq and Vietnam'. *Politics & Society* 35: 183–223.

Kalyvas, S. N. and N. Sambanis. 2005. 'Bosnia's Civil War: Origins and Violence Dynamics', in: *Understanding Civil War:*

Evidence and Analysis (edited by P. Collier and N. Sambanis). The World Bank, Washington, D.C., pp. 191–229.

Kaplan, R. 1993. *Balkan Ghosts: A Journey through History*. St. Martin's Press, New York.

———— 1997. 'Was Democracy Just a Moment?' *The Atlantic*. Available at http://www.theatlantic.com/magazine/archive/1997/12/was-democracy-just-a-moment/306022/ (accessed 30 January 2013).

———— 2000. *The Coming Anarchy: Shattering the Dreams of the Post Cold War*. Random House, New York.

Kaviraj, S. and S. Khilani (eds). 2001. *Civil Society: History and Possibilities*. University Press, Cambridge.

Keane, J. 2003. *Global Civil Society?* Cambridge University Press, Cambridge.

Keck, M. E. and K. Sikkink. 1998. *Activists Beyond Borders: Advocacy Networks in International Politics*. Cornell University Press, Ithaca, New York.

Keen, D. 1998. 'The Economic Functions of Violence in Civil Wars', in: *Adelphi Papers*. International Institute of Strategic Studies, London.

Kendall, J. and M. Knapp. 2000. 'The Third Sector and Welfare State Modernisation: Inputs, Activities and Comparative Performance'. In: LSE CCS Working Papers Collection, London.

Khilnani, S. 2001. 'The Development of Civil Society', in: *Civil Society, History and Possibilities* (edited by S. Kaviraj and S. Khilnani). Cambridge University Press, Cambridge, 11-33.

Kolind, T. 2007. 'In Search of Decent People: Resistance and Ethnicization of Everyday Life among Muslims of Stolac', in: *The New Bosnian Mosaic* (edited by X. Bougarel, E. Helms and G. Duijzings). Ashgate, London, pp. 123–40.

Kymlicka, W. 1996. *Multicultural Citizenship*. Oxford University Press, Oxford.

———— 2001. *Politics in the Vernacular: Nationalism, Multiculturalism and Citizenship*. Oxford University Press, Oxford.

———— 2007. *Multicultural Odysseys: Navigating the New International Politics of Diversity*, Oxford University Press, Oxford.

———— 2011. 'Transitional Justice, Federalism and the Accommodation of Minority Nationalism', in: *Identities in Transition: Challenges for Transitional Justice in Divided Societies* (edited by A. Paige), Cambridge University Press, Cambridge, pp. 303–33.

Large, J. 1997. *The War Next Door: A Study of Second-Track Intervention during the War in Ex-Yugoslavia*. Hawthorn Press, Stroud.

Lederach, J. P. 1997. *Building Peace: Sustainable Reconciliation in Divided Societies*. United State Institute for Peace Press, Washington, D.C.

———— 2001. 'Civil Society and Reconciliation', in: *Turbulent Peace: The Challenges of Managing International Conflict* (edited by C. Crocker, Hampson, F. O., & Aall, P.). United States Institute for Peace Press, Washington, D.C., pp. 841–54.

Lijphart, A. 1991. 'Constitutional Choices For New Democracies'. *Journal of Democracy* 2: 72–84.

———— 2004. 'Constitutional Design for Divided Societies'. *Journal of Democracy* 15: 96–109.

Locke, J. 1824. *Two Treatises on Government*. Printed for C. and J. Rivington, London.

Luttwak, E. N. 1995. 'Toward Post-Heroic Warfare'. *Foreign Affairs* 74: 109–22.

Maffettone, S. 2006a. 'Psiche e Polis', in: *La pensabilità del mondo, filosofia e governance globale*. Il Saggiatore, Milano.

———— 2006b. *La pensabilità del mondo, filosofia e governance globale*. Il Saggiatore, Milano.

———— 2010. *Rawls: An Introduction*. Polity Press, London.

Mamdani, M. 1996. *Citizens and Subjects*,

Contemporary Africa and the Legacy of Late Colonialism. Princeton University Press, Princeton, N.J.

May, S. T. Modood and J. Squires. 2004. *Ethnicity, Nationalism, and Minority Rights*. Cambridge University Press, Cambridge, UK.

McGraw, Bryan T. 2010. *Faith in Politics: Religion and Liberal Democracy*. Cambridge University Press, Cambridge.

Melander, E., M. Öberg and J. Hall. 2009. 'Are "New Wars" More Atrocious? Battle Severity, Civilians Killed and Forced Migration Before and After the End of the Cold War'. *European Journal of International Relations* 15: 505–36.

Min, B. and A. Wimmer. 2007. 'Ethnicity and War in a World of Nation-states', in: *The Cultures and Globalization Series 1: Conflicts and tensions* (edited by H. Anheier and Y. Isar), SAGE Publications, London, pp. 66–80.

Minow, M. 1998. *Between Vengeance and Forgiveness: Facing History After Genocide and Mass Violence*. Beacon Press, Boston.

Montesquieu, B. de. 1748 (1949). *The Spirit of the Laws*. 1748. Translated by Thomas Nugent. 2 vols. Hafner Press, New York.

Mosher, M. A. 1984. 'The Particulars of a Universal Politics: Hegel's Adaptation of Montesquieu's Typology'. *The American Political Science Review* 78: 179–88.

Nation, C. R. 2003. *War in The Balkans, 1991–2002*. US Army War College, Carlisle, Penn.

Obadare, E. 2004. 'The Alternative Genealogy of Civil Society and its Implication for Africa'. *Africa Development* 29: 1–8.

OECD-ORG. 2007. 'Trends in International Migration Flows and Stocks, 1975–2005'. In: OECD Social, Employment and Migration Working Papers. Organisation for Economic Cooperation and Development, Paris.

OHCHR (Office of the United Nations High Commissioner for Human Rights).

1976a. International Covenant on Civil and Political Rights (edited by UN). General Assembly Resolution 2200A (XXI), of 16 December 1966.

——— 1976b. International Covenant on Economic, Social and Cultural Rights (edited by UN). General Assembly Resolution 2200A (XXI), of 16 December 1966.

——— 1996. General Recommendation No. 21: Right to self-determination: 23/08/96. Gen. Rec. No. 21. (General Comments) (edited by UN). General Assembly A/51/18, in Agenda Item 108: Elimination of Racism and Racial Discrimination.

OHR. 1995. 'The General Framework Agreement for Peace in Bosnia and Herzegovina [Dayton Agreement]' (edited by O.O.T.H. Representative), Sarajevo.

Orjuela, C. 2003. 'Building Peace in Sri Lanka: A Role for Civil Society?' *Annual Review of Sociology* 40: 195–212.

Paffenholz, T. and C. Spurk. 2006. 'Civil Society, Civic Engagement, and Peacebuilding', in: Social Development Papers: Conflict Prevention and Reconstruction, n. 36, Washington, D.C.: The World Bank.

Parekh, B. 2002. *Rethinking Multiculturalism: Cultural Diversity and Political Theory*. Palgrave, London.

Paris, R. 2004. *At the War's End: Building Peace After Civil Conflict*. Cambridge University Press, Cambridge.

Parker, K. 2000. 'Understanding Self-determination: The Basics'. In: *First International Conference on the Right to Self-Determination*. UN, Geneva.

Pia, E. and T. Diez. 2007. 'Conflict and Human Rights: A Theoretical Frame-work', Luiss SHURwp1/07, available at http://shur.luiss.it/files/2009/06/piadiez.pdf (accessed 30 January 2013).

Pickering, M. P. 2006. 'Generating Social Capital for Bridging Ethnic Divisions in the Balkans: Case Studies of Two Bosniak

Cities'. *Ethnic and Racial Studies* 29: 79–103.

Pouligny, B. 2005. 'Civil Society and Post-Conflict Peacebuilding: Ambiguities of International Programmes Aimed at Building "New" Societies'. *Security Dialogue* 36: 495–510.

Powers, G. F. 1996. 'Religion, Conflict and Prospects for Reconciliation in Bosnia, Croatia and Yugoslavia'. *Journal of International Affairs* 50: 221.

Putnam, R. D. 1995. 'Bowling Alone: America's Declining Social Capital'. *Journal of Democracy* 6: 65–78.

Putnam, R. D. and S. J. Pharr (eds). 2000. *Disaffected Democracies, What's Troubling the Trilateral Countries?* Princeton University Press, Princeton, N.J.

Marchetti R., and Tocci N. (eds). 2011. *Conflict Society and Peace-building: The Role of Human Rights*, Routledge, New Delhi.

Ramsbotham, O. 2005. 'The Analysis of Protracted Social Conflict: A Tribute to Edward Azar'. *Review of International Studies* 31: 109–26.

Ramsbotham, O., T. Woodhouse and H. Miall. 2006. *Contemporary Conflict Resolution. The Prevention, Management and Transformation of Deadly Conflicts* [Second Edition]. Polity, Cambridge.

Rawls, J. 1971. *A Theory of Justice.* Harvard University Press, Cambridge, Mass.

——— 2000. *Lectures on the History of Moral Philosophy.* Harvard University Press, Cambridge, Mass.

——— 1993. *Political Liberalism.* Columbia University Press, New York.

——— 2005. *Political Liberalism* [Expanded Edition]. Columbia University Press, New York.

Richmond, O. and H. Carey. 2005. *Subcontracting Peace: the Challenges of NGO Peacebuilding.* Ashgate, Aldershot.

Rosenau, J. 1998. 'Governance and Democracy in a Globalizing World', in: *Re-Imagining Political Community: Studies in Cosmopolitan Democracy* (edited by D. Archibugi, D. Held and M. Kohler). University Press, Stanford, Calif., pp. 28–57.

Rosenblum, N. 2003. 'Civil Societies: Liberalism and the Moral Use of Pluralism' in: *Civil Society and Democracy* (edited by C. M. Elliott), Oxford University Press, New Delhi, pp. 106–14.

Rosenblum N. and R. Post (eds). 2002. *Civil Society and Government.* Princeton University Press, Princeton, N.J.

Rothman, J. 1997. *Resolving Identity-Based Conflict: In Nations, Organizations, and Communities.* Jossey-Bass Publishers, San Francisco.

Rothman, J. and M. L. Olson. 2001. 'From Interests to Identities: Towards a New Emphasis in Interactive Conflict Resolution'. *Annual Review of Sociology* 38: 289–305.

Rupesinghe, K. 1998. *Civil Wars, Civil Peace: An Introduction to Conflict Resolution.* Pluto, London.

Russett, B. M., J. R. Oneal and M. Cox. 2000. 'Clash of Civilizations, or Realism and Liberalism Deja Vu? Some Evidences'. *Annual Review of Sociology* 37: 583–608.

Sakbani, M. 2011. 'The Revolutions of the Arab Spring: Are Democracy, Development and Modernity at the Gate?' *Contemporary Arab Affairs* 4(2): 127–47.

Sambanis, N. 2001. 'Do Ethnic and Nonethnic Civil Wars Have the Same Causes? A Theoretical and Empirical Inquiry (Part 1)'. *Journal of Conflict Resolution* 45: 259–82.

Sandel, M. J. 1982. *Liberalism and the Limits of Justice.* Cambridge University Press, Cambridge.

——— 1996. *Democracy's Discontent: America in Search of a Public Philosophy.* Harvard University Press, Cambridge.

Seligman, A. B. 1992. *The Idea of Civil Society.* Princeton University Press, Princeton, N.J.

——— 2002. 'Civil Society as Idea and Ideal', in: *Alternative Conceptions of Civil So-*

ciety (edited by S. Chambers and W. Kymlicka). Princeton University Press, Princeton, N.J., pp. 13–33.

Sen, A. 1999. *Development As Freedom*. Oxford University Press, Oxford.

——— 2006a. *Identity and Violence: The Illusion of Destiny*. W. W. Norton & Company, New York, London.

——— 2006b. 'Democracy isn't "Western"'. *The Economist* (March). Available at http://online.wsj.com/article/SB1143171 14522207183.html (accessed 14 January 2013).

——— 2008. 'Violence, Identity and Poverty'. *Annual Review of Sociology* 45: 5–15.

Seul, J. R. 1999. 'Ours Is the Way of God: Religion, Identity, and Intergroup Conflict'. *Annual Review of Sociology* 36: 553–69.

Smith, A. 1776. *The Wealth of Nations*. In: *Adam Smith, Wealth of Nations* (edited by R. H. Campbell and A. S. Skinner). Oxford University Press, Oxford.

Stubbs, P. 1996. 'Nationalism, Globalization and Civil Society in Croatia and Slovenia. Reseach in Social Movements'. *Conflicts and Changes* 19: 1–26.

Taylor, C. 1994. 'The Politics of Recognition', in: *Multiculturalism* (edited by C. Taylor). Princeton University Press, Princeton, N.J., 25-74.

——— 1995. 'Invoking Civil Society', in: *Philosophical Arguments* (edited by C. Taylor). Harvard University Press, Cambridge, Mass.

Thoms, O. N. T. and J. Ron. 2007. 'Do Human Rights Violations Cause Internal Conflict?' *Human Rights Quarterly* 29: 674–705.

Tocqueville, de A. 1835/1840 (1994). *Democracy in America* (*De la Démocratie en Amérique; The Henry Reeve text*, edited by Phillips Bradley). David Campbell, Everyman's Library, London.

UN. 1994. 'Final Report of the Commission of Experts Established Pursuant to Security Council Resolution 780 (1992)'.

In: S/1994/674, 27 May 1994 (edited by U.N.S. Council).

——— 1948. 'Universal Declaration of Human Rights' (edited by UN). Adopted by General Assembly Resolution 217 A (III) of 10 December 1948.

Várady, T. 1997. 'Minorities, Majorities, Law, Ethnicity: Reflections of the Yugoslav Case'. *Human Rights Quarterly* 19: 9–54.

Varshney, A. 2001. 'Ethnic Conflict and Civil Society, India and Beyond'. *World Politics* 53: 362–98.

——— 2003a. *Ethnic Conflict and Civic Life: Hindus and Muslims in India*. Yale University Press, New Haven, Conn.

——— 2003b. 'Nationalism, Ethnic Conflict, and Rationality'. *Perspectives on Politics* 1: 85–99.

Wallensteen, P. and K. Axell. 1993. 'Armed Conflict at the End of the Cold War, 1989–92'. *Journal of Peace Research* 30(3): 331–46.

Wallensteen, P. and M. Sollenberg. 1999. 'Armed Conflicts, 1989–1998'. *Journal of Peace Research* 36(5): 604–5.

Waltz, K. 1959. *Man, the State and the War*. Columbia University Press, New York.

Walzer, M. 1995. *Toward a Global Civil Society*. Berghahn Books, Oxford.

——— 2003. 'The Idea of Civil Society: A Path of Social Reconstruction', in *Civil Society and Democracy* (edited by Carolyn M. Elliott). Oxford India Paperbacks, New Delhi: Oxford University Press, pp. 63–82.

Weiss, Joshua N. "Tuzla, the Third Side, and the Bosnian War." Third Side-Global Negotiation Project at University of Harvard (2004).

Wimmer, A., R. J. Goldstone, D. L. Horowitz, U. Joras and C. Schetter. 2004. *Facing Ethnic Conflicts: Toward a New Realism*. Rowman & Littlefield Publishers, INC, Oxford.

Woolcock, M. and D. Narayan 2000. 'Social Capital: Implications for Development

Theory, Research, and Policy'. *World Bank Res Obs* 15: 225–49.

Zubaida, S. 2001. 'Civil Society, Community and Democracy in the Middle-East', in: *Civil Society: History and Possibilities* (edited by S. Kaviraj and S. Khilnani). University Press, Cambridge, pp. 232–50.

Carta ecologica:
La carta che hai in mano è *Elementary Clorine Free*, cioè prodotta senza l'uso di cloro.
Il rispetto dell'ambiente significa qualità della vita.

LUISS *Sostenibile*
Associazione Culturale

Finito di stampare nel mese di febbraio 2013
Presso Prontostampa Srl
Via Redipuglia, 150 - 24045 Fara Gera D'Adda (BG)

CPSIA information can be obtained at www.ICGtesting.com
Printed in the USA
BVOW08s1929121115

426897BV00004BA/138/P